UN
SOCIAL MEDIA

Keep it Real!

*un*SOCIAL MEDIA

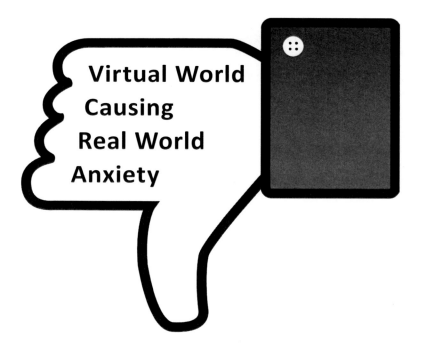

Virtual World
Causing
Real World
Anxiety

Wade Sorochan

Endorsed by the Mood Disorders Society of Canada

UNSOCIAL MEDIA
Virtual World Causing Real World Anxiety
Second printing

Copyright © Wade Sorochan, 2016, 2017

Edited by Kathy Salloum

Cover image © rclassenlayouts@123RF.com

Published by Wade Sorochan Communications, Edmonton, Canada

ISBN 978-1-988048-60-4

Library and Archives Canada Cataloguing in Publication

Sorochan, Wade, 1961-, author
 Unsocial media: virtual world causing real world anxiety / Wade Sorochan.

Includes index.
Issued in print and electronic formats.
ISBN 978-1-988048-60-4 (paperback).--ISBN 978-1-988048-61-1 (epub).
--ISBN 978-1-988048-62-8 (mobi)

 1. Social media. 2. Social media addiction. 3. Virtual reality--
Psychological aspects. 4. Stress (Psychology). 5. Technological
innovations--Psychological aspects. I. Title.

HM742.S67 2016   302.30285   C2016-904089-5
                                            C2016-904090-9

Publication assistance and digital printing in Canada by

PUBLISHING
PageMasterPublishing.ca

*To Char, Kendra, Linda
and my grandchildren*

In memory of that lost lonely little boy

Contents

Preface

This book is meant to be a resource guide on how social media could cause mental health issues. My goal is to bring awareness about how social media addiction can have negative effects on a person's mental health (especially those who are in a vulnerable state of mind) and recognize the real world emotions and feelings associated while in the virtual world. I share important information about mental illness and my personal story of my lifelong struggle with mental illness—being emotionally abused and abandoned as a child, living with high anxiety all my life, experiencing five mental breakdowns, eventually hitting rock bottom, and finally receiving treatment allowing me to be a mental illness survivor today. As a mental health advocate and motivational speaker, I am passionate about raising awareness about the importance of recognizing certain areas in life that could cause serious mental health issues: the effects of unmanaged stress and how the virtual world could cause real world anxiety. I have acquired extensive knowledge about the latest social media trends and have researched the connection between social media use and its effect on a person's mental health.

Studies now show that social media can actually make you feel sad, anxious and depressed. People will remain connected 24/7 for FOMO (fear of missing out), but what are they truly missing out on? Social media can become an anxiety induced fixation for "Likes" and "Comments." People will spend a great deal of time trying to take the "perfect selfie" to not show any flaws in their appearance. What is motivating people to share so much of themselves on social media? Is it a lack of self-esteem? Are people craving attention, looking for affirmation or acceptance in the virtual world that is maybe lacking in the real world? Many people believe that the virtual world will meet their emotional needs. The truth is only the real world can meet your emotional needs.

Introduction

Real world or virtual world; where do you live? Social media has blurred the line between the real world and virtual world. Nowadays it's rare to see someone looking up and experiencing the real world. People seem more interested in looking down at their smartphones to see what the virtual world has to offer. So what is the virtual world offering? I believe a better question to ask is *what is the virtual world causing?* Can social media cause mental health issues without us even knowing? Can we get so caught in something that we're not even aware of its negative effects on us?

Many people are experiencing high levels of anxiety and chronic fatigue due to social media addiction. It's causing poor academic and work performance, and serious mental and physical health issues. You will learn practical tips to cut social media addiction for all ages. This book will explain how descriptions like "Social" and "Friend" are not truly accurate, and how texting is causing a great deal of misunderstanding and bad feelings through miscommunication. You will learn about new terms like "Text Neck," "Phubbing," "Sharenting" and "Digital Kidnapping."

Today's youth only know a world that has the internet and cannot even imagine life without it. There's a virtual world of social networking sites and apps including: Facebook, Twitter, Instagram, Pinterest, Flickr, Snapchat and many others that allow users to pin, post, tag, chat, share, tweet, like and comment. I believe parents and educators have a responsibility to ensure that today's youth are aware of the negative effects of social media. You will acquire practical tools needed to open up a discussion on this important topic and discover that no matter what age you are, if you use social media and you're unaware of its negative effects, you could be at risk of developing mental health issues.

Social media is not all bad, but it can be addictive, and like any other addiction, it can be harmful or dangerous and potentially lead to *Social Media Anxiety*, possibly the next recognized mental health disorder. Think of this book as a warning label for an addictive drug.

CHAPTER ONE

Real World Stress

L et's first look at a major area in the real world that could cause mental health issues: STRESS. The Merriam-Webster's dictionary defines stress as "something that causes strong feelings of worry or anxiety." There are many stressors in life that can challenge our mental health and cause stress or anxiety: work, relationships, finances, physical health, change, trauma and many more. But does *technology* add more or less stress to our lives?

Technology: More or Less Stress?

alphaspirit@123RF.com

Today's technology provides a constant flow of information, causing interruptions and distractions to our daily lives. We are forced to emotionally and physically sift through all the information that is provided 24/7; with much of it horrific and disturbing. The internet is an unfiltered and uncontrolled global information network, forcing users to determine whether a news post is real or fake. According to a 2016 study by the Pew Research Centre, the majority of people (62%) get their news from social media.[1] Information comes in quicker now than ever before and can be extremely challenging and stressful trying to process it all. When the 9-11 attacks occurred, networks were getting calls from concerned parents asking them to stop replaying the moment the planes crashed into the World Trade Center Towers. The parents explained that their children were getting very upset, because every time there was a replay, the children believed more planes were crashing into buildings. It wasn't that long ago that if you wanted to be plugged in to current events, you would read the daily newspaper, listen to a five minute radio newscast, or tune in to the 6:00pm or 11:00pm television news. Between newspaper editions and broadcasts, you would live your life, not hearing about every disturbing detail.

Today, television news outlets commonly use video captured from viewer's smartphones, with the news anchor introducing a news story by saying "and it was all captured on video." We no longer see just the aftermath of a car accident, we now experience the accident as it happened through Dash Cam video; providing even more disturbing content.

If you choose to try to avoid today's fast-paced technology driven world and don't keep up with its advancements, you are looked at as someone who is "stuck in the past" and refusing to change. We all feel a certain amount of pressure to embrace new technology. It is imperative in today's

1. J.Gottfried, E.Shearer (May 26, 2016) News Use Across Social Media Platforms 2016. Pew Research Centre. Retrieved from: http://www.journalism.org/2016/05/26/news-use-across-social-media-platforms-2016/

workplace. Those who are unwilling or unable to adapt to technological change may miss out on employment advancements or may even be let go. It can be stressful learning new technologies. Many times it seems that when you learn a new system and develop a certain level of comfort operating that system, new technology arrives on the market and you start all over again in the name of technological "advancements."

A 2013 Huffington Post article showcased a number of studies in the UK on internet stress, including a 2011 University of Cambridge study that stated one in three workers are overwhelmed by technology and social media.[2] The study also found that technology-related stress was correlated with increased feelings of life dissatisfaction. In another study that surveyed 1,000 people, 38% of those surveyed said their stress levels would be higher if they were unable to use the internet as opposed to having utilities or television cut off. 27% of survey respondents said that they couldn't live without an internet connection, up from 17% the year before. The conclusion is: technology can be stressful but not having access to technology can also be stressful.

At work or at home, technology can be nerve-racking; keeping up with all your Facebook "friends," the demands of replying to text messages within five seconds, the addictive allure of posting cute and up-to-date photos of your family, having to keep up with status updates, and the FOMO (fear of missing out) on activities in the lives of friends and family. Social media also allows you to be more aware of stressful events in other people's lives.

2. Huffington Post (2013, April 15) *Internet Stress Tops Workers' List of Anxieties: Study.* Retrieved from: http://www.huffingtonpost.com/2013/04/15/internet-stress-tops-work_n_3084889.html

You used to have to have a personal connection with some-one to find out how they were doing, but now people are sharing everything online for all to see. You now feel an obligation to respond immediately, even though it may not be the best time for you. You may stress about how and when to respond.

The Pew Research Centre, a nonpartisan think tank based in Washington, D.C., conducted research to determine the degree to which technology use directly affects stress levels. The study found that awareness of stressful events in others' lives is a significant contributor to people's own stress. The study also found that those who are more educated and those who are married or living with a partner report lower levels of stress when it comes to social media use.[3] [4]

It's important to identify all the stressors in your life and develop effective strategies to deal with them. Nobody lives a completely stress free life. If anyone claims they are, chan-ces are they are not being totally honest with themselves and others. It's important to be open and honest about your mental health so you can identify issues before they become a serious mental health problem. It also allows you to receive support from friends and family and seek help if needed. Undealt with acute stress could lead to serious mental health issues like anxiety and depression. Everyone sees situations differently and has varying coping skills. For this reason, no two people will respond exactly the same way to any given situation.

3. Hampton, K. & Rainie L. & Lu,W. & Shin, I. & Purcell, K. (2015, January 15). *Social Media and the Cost of Caring*, Psychological Stress and Social Media Use. Retrieved from Pew Research Centre website: http://www.pewinternet.org/2015/01/15/-social-media-and-stress/

4. Hampton K. & Rainie, L. Lu,W. & Shin, I, & Purcell, K. (2015, January 15) *Psychological Stress and Social Media Use*. Retrieved from Pew Research Centre website: http://www.pewinternet.org/2015/01/15/psychological-stress-and-social-media-use-2/

A 2014 Statistics Canada study found that "23% of Canadians aged 15 and older (6.7 million people) reported that most days were *quite a bit* or *extremely* stressful." [5]

That's almost twenty five percent of the population admitting that "most days" they are not just a little bit—but "extremely" or "quite a bit" stressed. This is considered chronic stress which is defined as "a state of prolonged tension from internal or external stressors that may cause various physical, emotional or mental manifestations."

Chronic Stress:
Emotional, Mental and Physical Impact

Possible Emotional and Mental Impact

- Moodiness or *depression*
- Confusion
- Loss of sense of humour
- *Anxiety*
- Anger
- Irritability
- Fear
- Change in sleep patterns
- Change in weight or appetite
- Difficulty concentrating or making decisions
- Decreased memory
- Negative thinking
- Loss of interest
- Restlessness

---

5. Statistics Canada (2014, Jan.) *Perceived life stress* (Catalog No. 82-625-x). Retrieved from http://www.statcan.gc.ca/pub/82-625-x/2015001/article/14188-eng.htm

Possible Physical Impact

- Heart disease
- Increased risk of heart attack and stroke
- High blood pressure
- Ulcers
- Some types of bowel disease
- Damage to the immune system

The conventional wisdom is that unchecked acute stress may become chronic stress, and chronic stress could turn into a diagnosable mental disorder. It is important to effectively deal with the acute stress in your life before it becomes chronic and leads to mental health issues.

Tips to Cope With Stress

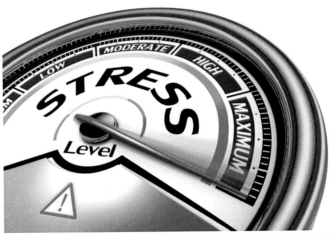

MICHAIL PANAGIOTIDIS@123RF.com

- Identify your problems and work on solutions
- Solve the little problems
- Talk about your issues
- Reduce tension

- Take your mind off your problems
- Try not to be too hard on yourself
- Make decisions
- Avoid putting things off
- Delegate
- Learn about stress management and relaxation techniques
- Maintain an overall healthy lifestyle

Good Stress?

Not all situations that are labeled stressful are negative; planning a wedding, buying a new home, job promotion, the birth of a child. All these are positive life events. Stress becomes a problem when we are not sure how to handle an event or a situation. Then worry sets in, and so does stress. Some situations in life are stress-provoking, but it is our thoughts that determine whether they are a problem to us. How we perceive a stress-provoking event and how we react to it determines its impact on our health. Strangely, we are not always aware that we are under stress. The habits, attitudes, and signs that alert us to problems may be hard to recognize because they have become so familiar. For many, it just becomes a way of life. But it's important to note that unmanaged stress can not only cause mental and physical problems, but it can also cause serious problems at home or at work. Seek help if you are unable to cope with stress. Talk to your healthcare provider.

Stress is a fact of life. No matter how much we might long for a stress-free existence, the fact is, stress is inevitable. Learning to manage stress can help you feel less tired and anxious, improve your quality of life and help you cope. Real world issues require real world solutions.

Online resources on stress awareness and management include:

Help Guide
www.helpguide.org

The Heart and Stroke Foundation
www.heartandstroke.com

CHAPTER TWO

Real World Mental Illness

lightwise@123RF.com

Most people are reluctant to discuss the topic of mental illness. I believe the main reason is lack of knowledge. Nobody feels comfortable or confident talking about any topic that they have little or no knowledge of. The more facts you know about mental illness, the more impact you have helping to break the silence and end the stigma surrounding it. There has been an increase in mental health awareness campaigns in the past few years. Success will be measured when there is a noticeable improvement in mental health services, and those who are suffering feel the tangible results of mental health campaigns. True success will also bring an end to the stigma, when mental illness is talked about and treated like any other illness, and like any other illness, if it goes untreated, can be fatal. The bottom line is: there is no health without mental health.

Mental Illness Facts

Information Leads to Hope and Hope Leads to Action

- 1 in 5 people will experience a mental illness in their lifetime — approximately 4.5 million Canadians and 61.5 million Americans (*Canadian Mental Health Association, National Alliance on Mental Illness*) [6] [7]

- Women are twice as likely to experience anxiety and depression as men (*Canadian Mental Health Association, Anxiety and Depression Association of America*) [8] [9]

---

6. Canadian Mental Health Association (2013). *Fast Facts about Mental Illness.* Retrieved from CMHA website: http://www.cmha.ca/media/fast-facts-about-mental-illness/

7. National Alliance on Mental Illness. (2015) *Mental Health By the Numbers.* Retrieved from: https://www.nami.org/Learn-More/Mental-Health-By-the-Numbers

8. Canadian Mental Health Association. *The Relationship Between Suicide and Mental Illness.* Retrieved from: http://toronto.cmha.ca/mental_health/the-relationship-between-suicide-and-mental-illness/

9. Anxiety and Depression Association of America. Retrieved from: http://www.adaa.org/living-with-anxiety/women

- Research indicates that the onset of anxiety and depression occurs earlier now in children than in past decades (*Rotter's Scale 1960-2002*) [10]

- Anxiety and depression continue to be Canada's fastest-rising diagnosis (*Statistics Canada*) [11]

- Mental disorders contribute more to the global burden of disease than all cancers combined (*Mood Disorders Society of Canada*) [12]

- Studies indicate a clear link between mental illness, addictions and substance abuse (*Centre for Addiction and Mental Health*) [13]

- Unemployment rate among people with serious mental illness: 70–90% (*Mood Disorders Society of Canada*) [14]

10. Gray, P. (2010, January 26) *The Decline of Play and Rise in Children's Mental Disorders.* Psychology Today. Retrieved from https://www.psychologytoday.com/blog/freedom-learn/201001/the-decline-play-and-rise-in-childrens-mental-disorders

11. Statistics Canada. *Canadian Community Health Survey: Mental Health, 2012.* Retrieved from: http://www.statcan.gc.ca/daily-quotidien/130918/dq130918a-eng.htm

12. Mood Disorders Society of Canada (2012) *Quick Facts: Mental illness and addiction in Canada.* Retrieved from Mood Disorders Society of Canada website: http://www.mooddisorderscanada.ca/documents/Media%20Room/Quick%20Facts%203rd%20Edition%20Eng%20Nov%2012%2009.pdf

13. Centre for Addiction and Mental health (2016) *Mental Illness and Addictions: Facts and Statistics.* Retrieved from http://www.camh.ca/en/hospital/about_camh/newsroom/for_reporters/pages/addictionmentalhealthstatistics.aspx

14. Mood Disorders Society of Canada (2012) *Quick Facts: Mental illness and addiction in Canada.* Retrieved from Mood Disorders Society of Canada website: http://www.mooddisorderscanada.ca/documents/Media%20Room/Quick%20Facts%203rd%20Edition%20Referenced%20Plain%20Text.pdf

- Mental illness is the number one cause of workplace disability (*Canada Safety Council/Centre for Addiction and Mental Health*) [15] [16]

- 500,000 Canadians miss work every day due to mental health issues (*Canadian Mental Health Association*) [17]

- Statistics have shown that over 60% of people with a mental health problem or illness won't seek help for fear of discrimination (*Mental Health Commission of Canada*) [18]

Five Truths About Mental Illness

By knowing the facts and talking openly and honestly about mental health, people start to believe these five basic truths about mental illness:

1. Mental illness is not a character weakness

2. It is not your fault

3. You are not alone

4. Mental illness is treatable

5. There is hope

15. Canada Safety Council. *Mental Health and the Workplace*. Retrieved from: https://canadasafetycouncil.org/workplace-safety/mental-health-and-workplace

16. Centre for Addiction and Mental Health. *Mental Illness and Addictions: Facts and Statistics*. Retrieved from: http://www.camh.ca/en/hospital/about_camh/newsroom/for_reporters/pages/addictionmentalhealthstatistics.aspx

17. Canadian Mental Health Association. *Mental Health for All Fact Sheet*. Retrieved form: http://mentalhealthweek.cmha.ca/files/2013/03/CMHA_MHW2012_Everyones_Concern_ENG_Final.pdf

18. Mental Health Commission of Canada. *Opening Minds*. Retrieved from: http://www.mentalhealthcommission.ca/English/initiatives-and-projects/opening-minds

A Survivor's Story

Things are not always what they seem. There are many people who are smiling on the outside, but crying on the inside. They say you can't judge a book by its cover. Let's look at my life's book cover. I have had a very successful career in broadcasting. My childhood dream of being on the radio came true right after high school. I was featured on the #1 rated talk show in Alberta, Canada, and became known as "The Tone Arm" — the first broadcaster in history to use music to enhance a radio talk show. Over the next 35 years I hosted a number of music radio programs, two more successful radio talk shows and a live interactive television talk show. I have been blessed to be able to maintain a long and successful career doing what I love. From looking at my life's book cover, many would assume that everything must be fine in my life. We really don't know what goes on inside the pages of someone's life book. The truth is that people are shocked to hear that I have had a lifelong struggle with anxiety and depression. I kept it hidden for most of my life.

I came from a broken home; my parents divorced when I was six. I was the youngest of four. The divorce caused division within the family. My oldest sister left with my father, and my other older sister wanted to leave, but was forced to stay with me and my older brother because she was too young. This caused plenty of tension in the household. My mother kept the three of us from having a relationship with our father and sister. When my mother remarried, I was eight years old and there was extreme pressure to develop a relationship with my stepfather. I did not feel closeness or any connection with him. I wanted to avoid him and my mother, so I spent many lonely hours in my bedroom watching TV or listening to music. My mother had control and anger issues that led to emotional abuse and abandonment. She didn't give me much attention as a child, except to criticize and reprimand. She could be very manipulative and hurtful. When we had guests in our home, she would force me to play the drums for the guests. I had no choice in the matter; I would end up playing the drums with tears rolling down my face. I felt like an object that she was controlling and showing off to others. Throughout my childhood if I didn't live up to her expectations (act a certain way, achieve a specific academic result), my mother would constantly ask "what's wrong with you?!"

Growing up I lacked love and affection and acceptance from my parents. I never experienced a nurturing hug or heard the words "I love you" or "don't worry, it will be OK." Not being assured that things were going to be OK made the world a very scary place for me. I experienced many anxiety induced panic attacks as a child that continued into my teen and adult years. Because of anxiety and depression, I've lived in fear with out-of-control worries most of my life, never at peace and not living in the moment.

Like any other child I needed guidance and nurturing, but unfortunately it was lacking to the point where I started to become very hyper, anxious and fearful about everything. I did not know how to control my emotions. Growing up I didn't have strong positive role models. I felt like an orphan, and many nights I would cry myself to sleep singing the song "Where is Love?" from the movie *Oliver*. High anxiety, extreme sadness and loneliness throughout most of my life has made it difficult to overcome adversity.

I was laid off in 1991, after 10 years of being on the radio. The station was trying to attract a buyer and wanted to reduce salaries. I was devastated that my first radio job had come to an end. I started to feel paralyzed with fear of the unknown and scared that I wouldn't be able to get another radio job. Even though I was a part of the most unique radio talk show in Canada, I was unable to attract attention from other stations in the market because none of them had a talk show format. I felt stuck and emotionally drained. I wasn't doing well at all. A friend suggested I go see a doctor. I didn't want to see a doctor because I didn't want people to label me as "crazy" or think that I couldn't handle it on my own. I didn't want to jeopardize my public image. As time went on I began to feel worse; high anxiety, extreme fatigue, hopelessness and low self-esteem. I reluctantly went to see my doctor and was diagnosed with Generalized Anxiety Disorder and Major Depression.

Anxiety

kbuntu@123RF.com

Anxiety is normal. Anxiety is hardwired into our brains. It is part of the body's fight-or-flight response, which prepares us to act quickly in the face of danger. It is a normal response to uncertainty, trouble, or feeling unprepared. However, if common everyday events bring on severe and persistent anxiety or panic that interferes with life, you may have an anxiety disorder.

Generalized Anxiety Disorder is the most common anxiety disorder. People with GAD worry excessively and uncontrollably about daily life events and activities, often expecting the worst even when there is no apparent reason for concern. They anticipate disaster and may be overly concerned about money, health, family, work, or other issues. This high-level anxiety makes normal life difficult and relaxation impossible.

Symptoms May Include:

- Irritability
- Feelings of dread
- Inability to control anxious thoughts
- Edginess or restlessness
- Inability to relax
- Panic attacks
- Difficulty sleeping and concentrating
- Fear of losing control or being rejected
- Muscle tension
- Aches or soreness
- Stomach problems
- Nausea
- Diarrhea
- Jumpiness or unsteadiness
- Fatigue
- Shakiness
- Sweating
- Headaches

Depression

Mood swings are normal. Small mood swings are a part of most people's lives. The normal ups and downs of life will cause sadness or the "blues" from time to time, but if symptoms persist, you may have depression.

Depression is the most common mood disorder that causes a persistent feeling of sadness and loss of interest. Also called Major Depressive Disorder or Clinical Depression, it affects how you feel, think and behave and can lead to a variety of emotional and physical problems. You may have trouble doing normal day-to-day activities, and sometimes you may feel as if life isn't worth living.

Symptoms May Include:

- Depressed mood
- Low energy
- Headaches
- Anger or irritability
- Appetite or weight change
- Changes in sleep patterns
- Anxiety
- Low self-esteem
- Loss of interest
- Fatigue
- Aches and pains
- Suicidal thoughts

It's important to note that symptoms could actually be other medical conditions (thyroid, cardiac issues, gastro issues, medication side effects, hormone issues, sleep problems, vitamin deficiencies), so getting a complete physical will help provide the correct diagnosis and treatment.

Suicide Awareness:
There Is Another Way

Untreated mental illness can ultimately end in death by suicide. Suicide occurs across all age, economic, social and ethnic boundaries. Suicide is the second leading cause of death among young people 10-24 (CMHA). Some people get so overwhelmed by unbearable emotional pain that the only way they see to end their pain is to end their life. Suicide is not necessarily about ending life, it's about ending pain. Unfortunately the pain doesn't end, it just transfers to others. Most people who attempt suicide want to live, but they become overwhelmed by unbearable emotional pain and can't see any other option.

Suicide *is* preventable.

Myths and Truths About Suicide

Myth: Young people rarely think about suicide

Truth: A Grade 7-12 survey revealed that:
    34% knew of someone
    16% seriously considered
    14% made a plan
    7% made an attempt
(2010 British Columbia study of 15,000 Grade 7 – 12 students) [19]

Myth: Talking about suicide will give a person the idea to consider suicide as a solution to their problem

Truth: Talking calmly without showing fear or making judgments can bring relief to someone who is feeling terribly isolated

It's important to take all threats or attempts seriously by responding in a direct straight forward manner. Do not try to solve the problem yourself, do not be sworn to secrecy, and do seek the assistance of a trained professional as soon as possible.

19. Canadian Mental Health Association, Toronto. *Some Myths About Suicide* Retrieved from: http://toronto.cmha.ca/mental_health/youth-and-suicide/

Possible Risk Factors:

- Being bullied
- Serious physical or mental illness
- Alcohol or drug abuse
- Family history of suicide
- History of trauma or abuse
- Major loss or life change
- Previous suicide threats
- Withdrawal
- Expressions of hopelessness

When it comes to mental illness the general rule of thumb is — if your thoughts, feelings or behaviors are significantly impairing your daily life, it may be time to seek help. Your family doctor is a good place to start.

Seek Help and Don't Give Up

My family doctor is where I started to seek help. He put me on a treatment program that included medication and therapy. Between 1991 and 2010, I fought my diagnosis. I would go off my treatment program when I was feeling better, but eventually I would crash again due to another job loss. I experienced five mental breakdowns in a 19 year period, each one getting progressively worse. The worst of all was in 2010 when I hit rock bottom. I realized I couldn't hide it anymore and I needed help. My serious crisis landed me in the hospital emergency room. I was immediately put under psychiatric care and enrolled in a three month intensive group therapy outpatient program. I committed to the program, but I thought if this doesn't ease my pain soon, I would start a plan to take my own life. I contemplated suicide while attending the group, but thankfully the treatment started to turn my thoughts towards living instead of dying. I started to think about the ripple effects of choosing death and how it would affect those I love. I then started to think about the ripple effects of choosing life and how that would allow me to enjoy family and friends and life in general. I also started to think about how my story could impact others who are suffering and offer them hope. I now know that I was fighting my diagnosis because I just wanted to be "normal" like everyone else. I realize now that everyone's "normal" is different. My "normal" is that I take medication and utilize strategies every day to help me function. I still struggle at times with high anxiety, depression, mental and physical exhaustion, and simple tasks can be overwhelming. I have to stay on my treatment program and use the learned strategies every day to deal with my mental illness. Mental illness is not curable, but it is treatable. If you stay on *your* treatment program, you should notice a difference in how you're feeling and functioning and others will notice as well. In the beginning it may take time to start feeling better, so DON'T GIVE UP.

Admitting I had a problem and seeking help was hard, but it was the best decision I have ever made for myself and my family. The tendency is to want to be alone in our suffering and not be a burden to others. The truth is that others care and want to help. We need to reach out and be honest with our friends and our healthcare provider about our feelings and emotions so we can receive the right treatment to get back on track. The earlier this can happen, the better. It's important to seek help as soon as possible because untreated mental health issues will affect your physical health as well.

Poor mental health equals poor physical health. In 2010, The Canadian Journal of Psychiatry published a study reporting that a person with mental illness had a 70 per cent higher mortality rate than the rest of the population.[20] It is not just death by suicide; it is diabetes, cancer and heart disease.

Untreated mental illness causes difficulties in all areas of life. It can ruin relationships, marriages and careers. It can ruin a life or ultimately end a life. It was a major contributing factor to my marriage breakdown. It can be very difficult living with someone who has mental illness. I respect my ex-wife for recognizing how I was affecting her and taking action to take care of her own mental health. A person living with someone who has a mental illness needs to be aware of how their own mental health is being affected. Everyone needs to take care of their own mental health first and foremost.

Online resources for mental illness and suicide awareness include:

The Canadian Mental Health Association
www.cmha.ca

Mood Disorders Society of Canada
www.mooddisorderscanada.ca

The Canadian Association for Suicide Prevention (CASP)
www.suicideprevention.ca

Help Guide
www.helpguide.org

---

20. Kisley, S. (2010) *Excess Mortality From Chronic Physical Disease in Psychiatric Patients — The Forgotten Problem*. The Canadian Journal of Psychiatry, 55, 749-751. Retrieved from https://espace.library.uq.edu.au/view/UQ:227010/UQ227010_OA.pdf

Unsocial Media

It's called social media, but how social is it? The Merriam-Webster definition of social is "relating to or involving activities in which people spend time *talking* to each other or doing enjoyable things *with* each other." According to this definition, social media is not social at all. We don't necessarily *talk* through social media; we are not *with* someone while on social media. We are usually *isolated* while on social media. Humans are inherently social beings. According to the Bible, after God created Adam, he realized that man should not be alone, so he created Eve. Now Adam had someone to socialize with. This story does have a social media connection — it was an "Apple" that Eve couldn't resist, and that obsession caused major problems!

People seem obsessed with social media. There's something about the virtual world that causes us to want to share pictures and comments with a feeling that we are "connecting" on some sort of "social" level. The postings on social media would not necessarily go over well in a real world situation. Imagine someone walking up to you at a social event, showing you pictures of their vacation without asking, or asking you to "like" their new dress or their plate of food. That wouldn't happen in the real world, but social media allows that to happen in the virtual world and people take advantage of it. People post whatever they want, convinced that others will find it interesting.

Social media is eroding people's real world social skills. Real world social skills require give and take, good body language and eye contact, a good listening ear and effective boundaries by knowing when to shut up! In the virtual world of social media, you can ramble all you want and post as many pictures as you want without anyone even asking to see your pictures or know your opinion. Social media allows us to be technologically connected but not socially connected. At least Skyping or FaceTime allows a live virtual social experience. This is especially beneficial for long distance relationships. It's important to balance online activity with real world activity. When often you see young people "socializing," most if not all are looking down at their phone rather than socializing with their friends. They are lacking social skills due to technology. Social skills are required for future relationships and job opportunities. Now for those who are socially awkward or shy (which are not mental illnesses), they may experience a level of connection and support through social media that they're unable to experience in the real world. For some that may be enough, but there are limitations to that type of connection. A virtual world connection can only go so far to meet emotional needs. People in long distance relationships can stay connected, but they are missing out on most aspects of a fulfilling relationship. Online dating sites are a good way to connect with people with similar interests, but it's important to note that those using online dating sites will eventually have to meet in the real world to see if that connection is truly real. So social media has its place, but it shouldn't replace face-to-face connections. Social media leads to isolation which could lead to mental health issues due to the lack of social and emotional connections.

The Dangers of Social Isolation

iqoncept@123RF.com

Everyone needs alone time; a time to gather your own thoughts without distraction. Everyone feels lonely sometimes — after a breakup with a friend or partner, death of a loved one, or a move to a new city. Chronic loneliness and social isolation can have many negative effects. We function best when our social needs are met. It's easier to stay motivated and deal with the challenges of life.

The effects of social isolation have been studied for years, and evidence shows that when our need for social relationships is not met, it can affect us mentally and physically. It can increase symptoms of anxiety and depression and cause poor physical health.

Psychologist John Cacioppo of the University of Chicago conducted a survey on the effects of loneliness.[21] [22] In the survey, doctors reported that they provide more complete medical care for patients who have supportive families and a healthy social circle. The survey also states that lonely and socially isolated individuals are at a higher risk for suicide. Loneliness and social isolation can raise stress hormones and blood pressure, creating a greater risk for heart disease. Humans are wired for social contact. Social interaction is vital for our mental and physical health. Social isolation can have serious life-threatening consequences.

Mental illness and isolation is not a good mix. If you are struggling with mental health issues and go online in isolation, there may be triggers that could cause you to feel more isolated and lonely, and increase mental illness symptoms. When isolated, your mind can take over and cause irrational thinking and negative thoughts. You may start to believe that no one cares and life is not worth living. If you're in need of emotional support and connection with a friend, only the real world can meet your emotional and social needs.

21. Cicioppo, J. Hawkley, L. (2010) *Loneliness, Health, and Mortality in Old Age: A National Longitudinal Study.* Retrieved from: http://www.ncbi.nlm.nih.gov/pmc/articles/PMC3303190/

22. Szalavitz , M. (2013, Mar. 3) *Social Isolation, Not Just Feeling Lonely, May Shorten Lives.* Retrieved from Time Magazine website: http://healthland.time.com/2013/03/26/social-isolation-not-just-feeling-lonely-may-shorten-lives/

"Phubbing"

Vadim Guzhva@123RF.com

It's quite common in social settings to notice people of all ages paying more attention to their cell phones than to the people around them, even to the extent of ignoring those closest to them. This can cause relationship problems and mental health issues.

The act of ignoring someone during a social interaction by looking at your phone instead of paying attention is referred to as "Phubbing." The term stems from a pairing of two words: phone and snubbing.[23] The origin of the word is attributed to a team of language experts who were recruited in a 2012 campaign by McCann Melbourne and Macquarie Dictionary in Australia. The term led to an online "Stop Phubbing Campaign" to draw attention to anti-social phone use. According to their website stop-phubbing.com, an average restaurant will see 36 cases of

---

23. Merriam-Webster. *Phubbing, An invented word that might be too useful to ignore.* Retrieved from: http://www.merriam-webster.com/words-at-play/phubbing-words-we're-watching

phubbing per dinner session, which is equal to spending 570 days alone, while in the company of others. The website also notes that 97% of people claim their food tasted worse while being a victim of phubbing. Experts believe the phubbing trend could lead to depression and relationship issues if not careful.

According to a 2015 survey of 453 adults by Baylor University in Texas, published by James A. Roberts, Ph.D. and Meredith David, Ph.D., 46.3% of respondents said their partners phubbed them by looking at their phones, and 22.6% said it "caused issues" in their relationship.[24] These lower levels of relationship satisfaction in turn led to lower levels of life satisfaction and ultimately higher levels of depression. To avoid phubbing someone or being phubbed yourself, simply be in the moment with the person you are with and turn off your mobile device.

Empathy Decline

According to a University of Michigan study of college students in the U.S. by Sarah Konrath at the Institute for Social Research, young people today have 40% lower empathy than their counterparts of 20 or 30 years ago.[25] The researchers examined 72 studies of students with a mean age of 20 from 1979 to 2000, all of whom had taken the Davis Interpersonal Reactivity Index test (IRI; Davis, 1980), a commonly used test designed to assess empath-

24. Baylor University (2015, September 29) *Cell Phones Can Damage Romantic Relationships, Leads to Depression*. Retrieved from Baylor University, Waco, Media Communications website: https://www.baylor.edu/mediacommunications/news.php?action=story&story=161554

25. Konrath, S. (2010, May 27) *Empathy: College students don't have as much as they used to*. Retrieved from the University of Michigan for News website: http://ns.umich.edu/new/releases/7724-empathy-college-students-don't-have-as-much-as-they-used-to

ic tendencies. *Psychology Today* defines empathy as "the experience of understanding another person's condition from their perspective. You place yourself in their shoes and feel what they are feeling. Empathy is known to increase prosocial (helping) behaviours." So *are* generation "Y" or "Millennials" really less empathetic? — and if so, what are the reasons? Researchers identify the influence of social media as a possible reason.

Dr. Tracy Alloway, an assistant professor of psychology at the University of North Florida studied adult Facebook users between ages 18 and 50, and found that some Facebook features are linked to selfishness.[26] [27]

The study revealed the one Facebook behavior that accurately predicted narcissism levels — the profile picture or selfie. The profile picture or a selfie allows narcissists to draw attention to themselves. According to The Mayo Clinic; "Narcissistic Personality Disorder is a mental disorder in which people have an inflated sense of their own importance, a deep need for admiration and a lack of empathy for others."

The researchers at the University of Michigan theorize that social media "creates a buffer between individuals making it easier to ignore others pain, or even at times, inflict pain upon others."

26. Alloway, T. & Runac, R. & Qureshi, M. & Kemp, G. (2014). *Is Facebook Linked to Selfishness? Investigating the Relationships among Social Media Use, Empathy, and Narcissism.* Social Networking, 3, 150-158. doi:10.4236/sn.2014.33020. Retrieved from: http://www.scirp.org/journal/PaperInformation.aspx?PaperID=45214

27. Arbor, A. (2013) *You're so vain: University of Michigan study links social media and narcissism.* Retrieved from University of Michigan for News website: http://www.ns.umich.edu/new/releases/21517-you-re-so-vain-u-m-study-links-social-media-and-narcissism

CHAPTER FOUR

Social Media Anxiety Disorder

sangoiri@123RF.com

Posting on social media is like putting yourself out there in the virtual world to be critiqued. During my live presentations, I usually ask for a volunteer to stand at the front, not say a word, and allow the crowd to critique them. To date I have had no volunteers. Standing up in front of a crowd is one of the top phobias people have. Most people would experience a high level of anxiety when putting themselves in that vulnerable position. So why are people so eager to post online to be virtually critiqued?

When you post something on social media you have a certain expectation of how many likes and comments you

would like to receive. So after you post online you anxiously wait for a response. Over a period of time you keep
checking to see how many "Likes" and "Comments" you
received. If it's not very many, you start to wonder why? So
you end up posting again and again and again, which turns
into a vicious cycle to achieve more likes and comments,
which can cause sadness, anxiety and depression.

Studies have shown that social media can make you feel sad,
anxious and depressed. According to a 2013 study by the
University of Michigan, the more people checked Facebook,
the more likely they were to feel worse about their own lives.[28]
The authors asked people to rate their level of life satisfaction
at the start and end of the two week study. They discovered
that the more participants used Facebook, the more their life
satisfaction levels declined. A 2012 study from Utah Valley
University found that many participants had the blues after
being on Facebook.[29] The more time they spent on Facebook,
the more likely they were to start thinking that their friends
lived better, happier lives. Another study in 2013 by German
researchers found that a third of people felt worse and
experienced feelings of resentment and envy after spending time on Facebook.[30] Researcher Hanna Krasnova from
the Institute of Information Systems at Berlin's Humboldt
University says the most common cause of envy was people

28. Kelly, H. (2013, August 15). *Using Facebook can make you sad.* Retrieved from CNN website: http://www.cnn.com/2013/08/15/tech/social-media/study-facebook-blues/

29. Chou, G. (2011, December) *"They are happier and having better lives than I am": the impact of using Facebook on perceptions of others' lives.* Cyberpsychology, Behavior, and Social Networking, 15, 117-121.doi: Retrieved from: https://www.researchgate.net/publication/51875201_They_Are_Happier_and_Having_Better_Lives_than_I_Am_The_Impact_of_Using_Facebook_on_Perceptions_of_Others'_Lives

30. Krasnova, H. & Wenninger, H. & Widjaja, T. & Buxmann, P. (2013, January 8) *Envy on Facebook: A Hidden Threat to Users' Life Satisfaction?* Retrieved from Humboldt University, Germany, Institute of Information Systems website: http://www.ara.cat/2013/01/28/855594433.pdf?hash=b775840d43f9f93b7a9031449f809c388f342291

comparing themselves to their peers, viewing vacation photographs causing the biggest resentment. Another common cause of envy came from the number of comments, likes and general feedback compared to friends.[31]

Before social media, friends would ask if you wanted to see their vacation photographs. Now you go online and BAM! There they are! They didn't even ask, but they're showing you anyway. It's like they're saying "I'm on vacation in this beautiful place...and you're not...IN YOUR FACE!!" Social media allows a platform for trying to impress other people.

The mental health effects of social media are now being seriously looked at and may identify the next anxiety disorder — "Social Media Anxiety Disorder" (SMAD). The term was used by Julie Spira, author, social media strategist and netiquette expert in a 2013 Huffington Post article.[32] Many experts believe social media anxiety needs to be included in the next edition of the *Diagnostic and Statistical Manual for Mental Disorders* (DSM).

Martha Bebinger, a reporter for radio station WBUR in Boston wrote an online article entitled Social Media Anxiety Disorder (SMAD): The Next New Medical Condition? [33] "Social Media Anxiety Disorder" is a syndrome that relates to Generalized Social Anxiety and Generalized Anxiety Disorder and is acquired when the participation of social media affects the mental and physical well-being of an individual.

---

31. Goldsmith, B. (2013, January 22). *Is Facebook envy making you miserable?* Reuters *RPT*. Retrieved from http://www.reuters.com/article/us-facebook-envy-idUSBRE90L0N220130122

32. Spira, J. (2013, Jan. 11) *Do you Suffer From Social Media Anxiety Disorder?* [Blog post]. Retrieved from Huffington Post website: http://www.huffingtonpost.com/julie-spira/social-media-anxiety_b_2451439.html

33. Bebinger, M. (2012, April 10). *Social Media Anxiety Disorder (SMAD): The Next New Medical Condition?* WBUR Boston. Retrieved from: http://commonhealth.wbur.org/2012/04/social-media-anxiety-disorder

Symptoms May Include:

* Feeling a sense of attachment to your phone or computer as if nothing else matters more.
* Spending eight or more hours a day browsing social networking sites.
* Frequently checking the number of followers or likes and comments on social networking sites and constantly finding opportunities to increase response.
* Built up anxiety when you don't receive an expected amount of "Likes" or "Comments."

The Effects on Your Mental Health May Include:

* Clingy behaviour — always seeking to please people
* Extreme loneliness
* Low self-esteem
* Body image issues
* Dysfunctional families
* Mistaking the virtual world for the real world

In 2014, Sheknows.com conducted a unique week-long workshop helping students realize the impact of social media on them.[34] The teens didn't think that Facebook, Instagram and Snapchat added much extra anxiety to their lives. They didn't really give much thought to the notion that social media can impact people emotionally until there was a discussion about its psychological effect. When the conversation turned to the importance of "Likes" and the FOMO (fear of missing out), the teens admitted they were definitely familiar with the feeling. I believe parents and educators need to have this discussion with young people

34. Wallace, K. (2014, Nov. 20). *Teen "Like" and "FOMO" anxiety.* CNN. Retrieved from CNN website: http://www.cnn.com/2014/10/16/living/teens-on-social-media-like-and-fomo-anxiety-digital-life/

to make them more aware of the negative emotional effects of social media and to identify the feelings and emotions associated with it.

Here are some good questions for parents and educators to ask youth:

- What is your main motivation for posting on social media?
- Are you often satisfied with the number of responses to your posts?
- Have you experienced anxiety (which became a distraction in your daily life) waiting for responses to something you posted on social media?
- Have you ever felt anxious, sad, depressed or experienced low self-esteem when you did not receive an expected amount of likes or comments?
- Do you have a fear of missing out? (what are you missing out on and how does it impact your life?)
- Do you feel that your emotional and social needs are being met on social media?

It's important to identify any triggers that cause you to gravitate towards social media. Before you go online ask yourself these questions — what is my motivation for going online? Am I seeking validation? Am I lonely? Am I sad? Is it low self-esteem? Am I looking for affirmation, acceptance or craving attention? These are good questions to ask yourself before going into the virtual world. You may end up feeling worse, research has shown that. Talk to someone in the real world if you're feeling down. Only the real world can meet your emotional needs.

Me, My Selfie and I

juliatim@123RF.com

In this world of digital photography, we can take as many pictures as we want and preview them before posting on Instagram, Facebook, Snapchat, or other sites. Back in the day we would take two pictures, wait and hope they turned out. Plus there was no such thing as a "selfie." We pointed the camera away from us towards other people or things. If we wanted to take a picture of ourselves, we would ask someone to take it. At one time the selfie was limited to the length of your arm. Now there is the "selfie stick." You can now extend the camera to include many people in your selfie. But that's not a selfie — that's a "Groupie!" The selfie stick is banned in most museums and even on rides at Disneyland because of the potential danger to people and items. People are even using a selfie stick while riding in cars or on motorcycles. That would be just like jousting. Didn't we learn anything from the medieval times? Nowadays it seems people take more pictures of themselves than any-thing else. It becomes the quest for the perfect selfie.

Selfie and Self-esteem

There are many tutorials online on how to create the "perfect" selfie. A lot of time is spent on getting the right angle, proper lighting, and the perfect facial expression. You can blame celebrities on this one. If a celebrity is posing with a certain facial expression, all of a sudden it becomes an online trend with many trying to emulate it. People will do the "Duck Face;" a term used to describe the face made if you push your lips together in a combination of a pout and a pucker, giving the impression you have larger cheekbones and bigger lips. There is also the "Fish Gape," where your face is slightly relaxed, mouth opened slightly, teeth visible and there is a slight squinting of the eyes. The selfie craze also includes full body photos in front of a mirror. Certain celebrities receive a lot of attention by posting nude or nearly nude "mirror selfies." In a disturbing trend, girls who are influenced by celebrities are now doing the same.

Many virtual world images are not real. They have been doctored to look as perfect as possible. This is similar to magazine covers of beautiful people that are airbrushed to look perfect. But unfortunately, many young people will buy into it and try to create that perfect image for themselves. They will spend a great deal of time trying not to show any perceived flaws in their appearance. When they think they have created the perfect image, they post it online and anxiously wait for responses.

As mentioned earlier, most people would not enjoy being critiqued in the real world, yet they are willing to be critiqued in the virtual world, which could lead to low self-esteem, body image issues and mental health problems. There are healthcare professionals who are concerned that the rise of selfies could influence the rise of Body Dysmorphic Disorder (BDD). According to the Mayo Clinic, Body Dysmorphic Disorder is a mental disorder in which a person intensely obsesses about perceived flaws in their appearance — flaws that, to others, are either minor or not observable. People with BDD constantly seek reassurance, and can spend many hours a day grooming and checking mirrors, causing significant distress and impact on their daily lives. Alarming new research by the child advocacy group Common Sense Media shows more than half of girls and one-third of boys as young as six to eight years old think their *ideal* body is *thinner* than their current body size. By age seven, one in four kids has engaged in some kind of dieting behavior.[35] [36]

The latest social media obsession for teens is called "The 100 Club." Teens post a picture on Facebook or Instagram and try to achieve at least 100 "Likes." [37] This competition puts a lot of pressure on teens and can cause high anxiety. As mentioned earlier, teens who do not receive the amount of likes they expect will feel anxious, sad, depressed and experience low self-esteem. So they end up posting again and again to try to get more likes, which just adds to the anxiety.

35. Common Sense Media (2015, Jan. 21). *Children, Teens, Media, and Body Image*. Retrieved from: https://www.commonsensemedia.org/research/children-teens-media-and-body-image

36. Wallace, K. (2015, Feb. 23) *Kids as young as 5 concerned about body image*. CNN. Retrieved from: http://www.cnn.com/2015/02/13/living/feat-body-image-kids-younger-ages/#

37. *"The 100 Club" is the latest social media obsession for teens that is also likely causing anxiety. (2014, October 27)* Retrieved from http://abc7.com/society/social-media-100-club-new-obses-sion-for-teens/368928/

The Quest for "Friends"

Everyone likes to have friends; friends to share special moments with, to offer help when needed and provide comfort and support through difficult times. Merriam-Webster's dictionary defines friend as "a person who you like and enjoy being with." Social media allows us to have hundreds of "friends" or "followers," but how many are genuine friends who fit the definition? According to recent research from Oxford University, even though the average Facebook user in the study has 155 friends, they consider only 28% of their Facebook friends to be genuine friends.[38] [39] [40] When asked how many of their Facebook friends they could go to for sympathy, the answer was 14. When asked how many they could turn to for support in a crisis, the answer was 4. The survey questioned more than 3300 social media users to see if using social media really means having more friends. Professor Robert Dunbar, who carried out the survey, says "no amount of social media will prevent a friend eventually becoming just another acquaintance if you don't meet face-to face from time to time — which is crucial for maintaining friendships." [41]

The research proves that social media creates a virtual society of *acquaintances* with only a handful of *real*

38. University of Oxford (2016, Jan. 20) *How face-to face still beats Facebook.*
Retrieved from: http://www.ox.ac.uk/news/2016-01-20-how-face-face-still-beats-facebook-0

39. Knapton, S. (2016, Jan. 20) *Facebook users have 155 friends - but would trust just four in a crisis.* The Telegraph. Retrieved from: http://www.telegraph.co.uk/news/science/science-news/12108412/Facebook-users-have-155-friends-but-would-trust-just-four-in-a-crisis.html

40. Williams, C. (2016, Jan. 25) *Only 4 Of Your Facebook Friends Really Matter, New Study Finds: Your Facebook friend count is a sad, empty lie.* Huffpost Tech. Retrieved from: http://www.huffingtonpost.com/entry/your-facebook-friend-count-is-a-sad-empty-lie_us_56a66278e4b0d8cc109ad9ba

41. Dunbar R. (2016 Jan.20) *Do online social media cut through the constraints that limit the size of offline social networks? DOI: 10.1098/rsos.150292*
Retrieved from: http://rsos.royalsocietypublishing.org/content/3/1/150292

friends. Facebook and other social networking sites don't distinguish between close and more distant friends — even though there is a clear distinction in the real world.

Some suggest Facebook should have an "acquaintance" category to identify different types of friendships. When Facebook first came out with the word "friend," I questioned the use of that word. I think a more appropriate word for a social media friend would be "STALKER." Merriam-Webster's definition of stalk is "to follow, watch, and bother constantly." Food for thought.

CHAPTER FIVE

Communication Breakdown

iqoncept@123RF.com

Texting: A Popular Way of Communicating

Texting has become a popular way of communicating FYI (for your information). It's a time saver. You don't have to find time or spend time talking to someone, you are in complete control of sending and responding to text messages. NRN (not right now). You don't even have to spend much time texting a message. Words are abbreviated and acronyms are used to save time and keep messages as short as possible. But be aware of autocorrect which can change the meaning of your text. A friend of mine was in the drive thru getting a coffee and she decided to text her husband to see if he wanted her to pick him up a hot chocolate. So she texted "would you like me to pick you up a hot choc?" Autocorrect changed it to "would you like me to pick you up a hot *chick?*"

There's an acronym for just about any phrase you want. UGTBK (you've got to be kidding). Texting is here to stay...IIWII (it is what it is) and for parents it may be the main way of communicating with older children. Be aware of acronyms that have changed over the years. LOL is no longer Lots of Love, it's Laugh out Loud. Don't text a friend who just lost his or her job "sorry to hear about your job loss LOL." Sometimes abbreviating words can go too far. People are now shortening OK with just K. I like to respond with "Potassium back to you." Texting allows people to really stretch the truth. When people respond with ROFL (rolling on the floor laughing), that's not true. Would they really do that when they are with another person who makes them laugh? — NO! So I created a more accurate acronym response to a funny post — SC (slight chuckle).

Definition of Communicate

The Merriam-Webster's definition of communicate is "to get someone to understand your thoughts or feelings." When it comes to texting, one person put it this way: "Texting is a brilliant way to miscommunicate how you feel, and misinterpret what other people mean." Growing up, communication was rarely misunderstood because we talked directly to each other with not only words but tone of voice and body language. When your friend, a parent or a teacher told you something, you knew exactly what they meant.

Elements of Effective Communication

Words make up only 7% of effective communication. Body language makes up 55% and voice tone and modulation makes up 38%. Texting is missing out on 93% of effective communication. It's no surprise that texting is causing a lot of miscommunication. Face to face communication is always the best because it creates a social connection, which you can't create by only texting. The words "I am sad" or "I love you" have much more of an impact face to face and you are more likely to experience a genuine social connection to meet your emotional needs.

Instant Gratification and Impatience

icetray@123RF.com

Texting is also causing anxiety due to a *high expectation* to receive an *immediate* response to a text. After sending a text, if a response doesn't arrive immediately, you start to get anxious and think that person must be mad at you. So you send another text asking "did you get my text?" and this time you end the text with a happy face emoji. Now they have a right to get mad at you! Just maybe they were busy at the time doing something important in the *real world*. The same applies when you call someone on their cell phone: you expect them to answer right away. Some actually do answer right away. I've seen it at the grocery store. People will literally drop everything while fumbling around trying to find their phone to answer it before it goes to voice mail. We all know that when the call is answered, the same annoying questions will follow — "where are you and what are you doing?"

In a 2013 Boston Globe article written by Christopher Muther, he writes about a study by the Pew Research Center's Internet & American Life Project how instant gratification is making us perpetually impatient and anxious.[42] Instant gratification is the desire to experience fulfilment without delay. Basically, it's wanting something — and wanting it now. The demand for instant results is seeping into every corner of our lives. We want same-day delivery services. We want stores and services available 24 hours a day. We don't want to wait for our favorite television program to air, so we subscribe to on demand TV. Smartphone apps now eliminate the wait for a bus or a table at restaurant. We want news when we want it, so we download apps that alert us on every news event happening at that particular moment. But experts caution that instant gratification comes at a price: it's making us less patient. The Pew

---

42. Muther, C. (2013, Feb. 2) *Instant gratification is making us perpetually impatient.* Retrieved from: https://www.bostonglobe.com/lifestyle/style/2013/02/01/the-growing-culture-impatience-where-instant-gratification-makes-crave-more-instant-gratification/q8tWDNGeJB2mm45fQxtTQP/story.html

Research Center's Project sums up their study about people under the age of 35 and the dangers of their hyper connected lives with what sounds like a prescription drug warning: "Negative effects include a need for instant gratification and loss of patience." We've come to expect things so quickly that researchers found people can't wait more than a few seconds for a video to load. Ramesh Sitaraman, a computer science professor at University of Massachusetts Amherst, examined the viewing habits of 6.7 million internet users in a study released in 2012.[43] How long were subjects willing to be patient? — two seconds. "After that they started abandoning," Sitaraman said. "After five seconds, the abandonment rate is 25%. When you get to ten seconds, half are gone."

The desire for instant gratification puts pressure on everyone — from the person making your latte to major corporations. Experts warn that the need for instant gratification could lead to acting on temptation and possibly cause addiction. Instant gratification could also have a serious impact on relationships. People in relationships could become overly impatient with each other when needs are not met instantly. So what are we missing out on by wanting something and wanting it now? We are missing out on the benefits of delayed gratification, which maximizes the pleasure by combining the anticipation with the actual receiving. What ever happened to patience is a virtue or good things are worth waiting for? As a kid, I remember the anticipation for something was just as exciting as receiving it!

43. Sitaraman, R. K. & Krishnan S.S. (2012) *Video Stream Quality Impacts Viewer Behavior: Inferring Causality Using Quasi-Experimental Designs.* Retrieved from:
http://ieeexplore.ieee.org/xpl/login.jsp?tp=&arnumber=6616025&url=http%3A%2F%2Fieeexplore.ieee.org%2Fiel7%2F90%2F4359146%2F06616025.pdf%3Farnumber%3D6616025

Chapter Six

Technology and Pornography

Technology has made it easier than ever to access pornography. A simple online search can result in thousands of sexually explicit images and videos. Pornography addiction is much more common than most people think, and it is on the rise. A 2014 survey of young Canadians conducted by MediaSmarts revealed more teens are actively seeking pornography online, compared to the results of a similar survey released in 2005.[44] They surveyed 5,436 students in grades 4 through 11 in every province and territory. Questions about sexuality were limited to older students in grades 7-11. The survey shows that boys are most likely to search for online pornography. 40% of teen boys admitted to searching for pornography in the past year, with 14% of them looking for pornography online at least once a day, and 14% once a week. That compares to 7% of girls who have searched for online pornography.

An organization called GuardChild has researched and compiled a list of Child Internet Crime and Abuse Statistics from: The Pew Institute, The National Crime Prevention Center, The University of New Hampshire, Youth Internet Safety Survey, The National Center for Missing and Exploited Children, Crimes Against Children Resource Center, Child Exploitation and Online Protection, Psychologies Magazine,

---

44. MediaSmarts (2014) *Sexually and Romantic Relationships in the Digital Age*. Retrieved from: http://mediasmarts.ca/sites/mediasmarts/files/pdfs/publication-report/full/YCWWIII_Sexuality_Romantic_Relationships_Digital_Age_FullReport_0.pdf

Project Tomorrow, FBI, Cox Communications and other resources.[45]

Some of the results include:

- 70% of children 7 to 18 years old have accidentally encountered online pornography
- 90% of children ages 8-16 have seen online pornography
- The largest group of internet pornography consumers is children ages 12–17

Lynn Margolies, Ph.D. says children's curiosity may cause them to search online about sex, and that most children and teens do not suffer from sex addictions. She goes on to say that sex addiction is usually secondary to other hidden issues in the family affecting them, which must be the focus of treatment. Viewing pornography on an ongoing basis can have potentially detrimental effects on children. Being introduced to images of sex before the child has a complete understanding about healthy sexuality, which includes relationship, responsibility and intimacy, will confuse the child and create an inaccurate model of adult sexual behavior. The detachment of the emotional connection of sex will have detrimental effects on future relationships.

Many marriages are in crisis or have ended because of pornography addiction. Pornography portrays women as sex objects. Men who are addicted to pornography may put pressure on their partner to emulate the staged online sex. Pornography can lead to sexual objectification — the act of treating someone as an object rather than as a whole

45. GuardChild. (2009) *Internet Statistics*. Retrieved from: http://www.guardchild.com/statistics/#sthash.DPHegYV3.dpuf

person. Addiction to pornography and frequent masturbation could lead to erectile dysfunction, which could cause serious relationship problems and mental health issues. Whether you're a teen or an adult, you need to recognize your addiction and how it's affecting you and those around you, and seek help immediately by talking to a professional addictions counselor.

Tips for Parents in Dealing with Pornography [46]

Remain Calm

Use a neutral and nonjudgmental tone in talking to teens, taking care not to lecture, yell, blame or shame them for their behavior or for hiding it.

Be Frank and Upfront

Let them know you are aware that they have been looking at some websites that can be confusing and harmful to children.

Explain the Dangers

- You can easily get addicted to viewing these images because they trick you into feeling pleasure and excitement. You may not realize it until it's too late. Once you get addicted you feel compelled to keep doing it, you aren't in control and it's hard to stop.

- The images can be sexually exciting and that can make you want more and more. Eventually the things

---

46. Margolies,L. (2015, Oct. 30) *Teens and Internet Pornography.* Retrieved from: http://psych-central.com/lib/teens-and-internet-pornography/

that would naturally create sexual excitement will no longer have that effect.

- Going to these sites can make you feel ashamed and bad about yourself and then you have to hide this behavior from people.

- The images will mislead you. You won't be able to tell what's normal sexual behavior and what isn't.

- Viewing these images repeatedly can have negative effects on development of healthy sexuality and that will affect your relationships in the future.

"Sexting"

Another dangerous activity that technology is facilitating today is called "sexting." The first published use of the term sexting was in a 2005 article in the Australian Sunday Telegraph Magazine (a combination of the words sex and texting). Sexting refers to the sending, receiving, or forwarding of sexually explicit or suggestive images, videos or messages by cell phone or any other mobile device. Research on sexting was conducted by The National Campaign to Prevent Teen Pregnancy, The Pew Internet & American Life Project, and the Cox Communications Teen Online & Wireless Safety Survey.[47] [48] [49] The research reveals that 1 in 5 teens have engaged in sexting by sending, receiving, or forwarding

47. GuardChild (2009) *Teenage Sexting Statistics*. Retrieved from: http://www.guardchild.com/teenage-sexting-statistics/

48. Schwartz, D. CBC News. (2014, May. 29) *Sexting, pornography findings in youth survey a new warning*. Retrieved from: http://www.cbc.ca/news/health/sexting-pornography-findings-in-youth-survey-a-new-warning-1.2657708

49. Cox Communications, National Center for Missing & Exploited Children® (NCMEC) and John Walsh (2009). *Teen Online & Wireless Safety Survey; Cyberbullying, Sexting, and Parental Controls*. Retrieved from: http://www.cox.com/wcm/en/aboutus/datasheet/takecharge/2009-teen-survey.pdf

sexually explicit nude or semi-nude photos (65% girls, 35% boys). Sexting occurs mostly in older teens (61% ages 16–18, 39% ages 13–15). Most sexting occurs between boyfriends and girlfriends, but in a disturbing finding 11% of teens sexted pictures to people they don't even know. 38% of teens say exchanging sexually suggestive content makes dating or hooking up with others more likely and 29% of teens believe those exchanging sexually suggestive content are "expected" to date or hook up.

24/7 access to pornography, sexting and media images pushing the boundaries are all contributing to girls becoming hyper-sexualized and it's happening at an earlier age than ever before. Certain celebrities have enjoyed their most success after sexualizing themselves through sexually seductive clothing and behavior. It seems the message that girls are getting today from pop culture and social media is that you need to draw attention to yourself – and the sexier the better.

Nude or sexually suggestive photos have the potential to spread to hundreds of people in a matter of seconds, which could cause feelings of guilt, shame, humiliation and embarrassment and can lead to public ridicule, bullying and serious mental health issues. In the case of a relationship break-up, the explicit photos could be used for vengeful purposes and put out there in the virtual world for all to view. 25% of teen girls and 33% of teen boys say they have had nude or semi-nude images originally meant for someone else shared with them. The photos could haunt a teen for the rest of his or her life affecting future college and job opportunities. And even more serious are the legal consequences. In Canada and some States a teen could face felony charges under child pornography laws for sending or forwarding sexually explicit photos of children under the age of 18, and may be required to register as a sex offender.

75% of teens admit that sending sexually suggestive content can have serious negative consequences. So why do they do it? Some teens see it as "normal" behavior. Teens use it as a way of flirting or as a joke or to be popular. The research reveals that 12% of teen girls felt pressured to send sexually suggestive messages or images. 23% of teen girls and 24% of teen boys say they were pressured by friends to send or post sexual content. Sexting can damage a youth's self-esteem and could lead to depression or other serious mental health issues.

Acronyms Parents Need to Know

There are certain acronyms that are being used by young people that can lead to risky behavior. Here's a sample of some, but be aware that acronyms are changing quickly with new ones constantly being added.

GNOC	Get Naked on Cam
IWSN	I Want Sex Now
8	Oral Sex
LMIRL	Let's Meet in Real Life
CU46	See You for Sex
MorF	Male or Female?
TDTM	Talk Dirty to Me

DOC	Drug of Choice
GYPO	Get Your Pants Off
CD9	Code 9 - Parents are Around
LHSO	Let's Have Sex Online
LHU	Let's Hook Up

Kids Health offers advice for parents on how to teach their teens about the dangers of sexting.[50]

- Talk to your child about the realities of posting online. What seems temporary may actually be permanent in the virtual world and shared numerous times to just about anyone in the world. Once an image is sent, it is no longer in their control, it can't be taken back. Follow the WWGT rule — what would Grandma think?

- Have open conversations about personal responsibility, boundaries, and how to resist peer pressure.

- Make it clear that there will be consequences if they are caught sexting.

---

50. Kids Health. *Sexting: What Parents Need to Know.* Retrieved from: http://kidshealth.org/en/parents/2011-sexting.html#

CHAPTER SEVEN

Heads Up!

Oleg Dudko@123RF.com   Francisco Juan Marin Terroba@123RF.com

The Dangers of Distracted Walking and Driving

We live in a time when almost everyone is looking down at their mobile devices while standing, walking and even driving. All are hazardous to your health — lack of emotional connections, harm or death when walking or driving. Think of this — a texting driver is twenty-three times more likely to get into a crash than a non-texting driver. Drivers typically spend nearly five seconds looking at their mobile phones. When traveling at a typical highway speed, that's enough time to cover the length of a football field blind-folded (Virginia Tech Transportation Institute).[51] [52] The simple answer is; don't use your phone while driving. Even hands

51. Box, S. (2009) *New data from Virginia Tech Transportation Institute provides insight into cell phone use and driving distraction.* Retrieved from
http://www.vtnews.vt.edu/articles/2009/07/2009-571.html

52. Lohmann, R. (Sept, 2012) *Texting and Driving: A Deadly Decision The dangers of teen texting while driving.* Psychology Today. Retrieved from: https://www.psychologytoday.com/blog/teen-angst/201209/texting-and-driving-deadly-decision

free devices are a distraction. Even though many jurisdictions have distracted driving laws, many drivers are still choosing to use their device while driving and putting themselves and others at risk. According to the National Safety Council, one out of every four car accidents in the United States is caused by texting and driving.[53]

According to the Virginia Tech Transportation Institute, texting while driving is six times more likely to cause an auto crash than driving when intoxicated. According to the Institute for Highway Safety Fatality Facts, 11 teens die every day as a result of texting while driving. In a poll conducted by the AAA, 94% of teen drivers acknowledge the dangers of texting and driving, but 35% admitted to doing it anyway.[54] Is a text or a phone call worth more than your life?

Distracted walking could also cause injury and possibly death. With people having their head down looking at their phone and not paying attention to their surroundings, they are putting themselves and others in danger. It is referred to as being a "petextrian." [55] It's become such a big problem that the National Safety Council has officially added cell phone distracted walking to its annual report of unintentional injuries and deaths. According to a 2010 study by the University of Ohio, injuries related to walking while using a cell phone doubled between 2005 and 2010, and the percentage of pedestrians killed while using cell phones has risen from less than 1% in 2004 to more than

---

53. National Safety Council (2013) *Annual Estimate of Cell Phone Crashes 2013*. Retrieved from: http://www.nsc.org/DistractedDrivingDocuments/Attributable-Risk-Estimate.pdf

54. Snyder, E. & Associates *Cell Phone Use While Driving Statistics*. Retrieved from https://www.edgarsnyder.com/car-accident/cause-of-accident/cell-phone/cell-phone-statistics.html

55. Dooley, E. (2015, Aug.10) *Distracted Walking: How 'Petextrians' Are Endangering Our Streets* ABC News, Retrieved from: http://abcnews.go.com/US/distracted-walking-petextrians-endangering-streets/story?id=32990067

3.5% in 2010.[56] In a 2012 pedestrian texting study by the University of Washington, pedestrians who text are four times less likely to look before crossing the street, cross in crosswalks, or obey traffic signals. Another study conducted by the University of Birmingham found that students using cell phones took up to 20% longer to cross the street than students who were not using a cell phone.[57] [58] According to a 2016 poll conducted in Canada by market research company Insights West, 66% of people surveyed would support legislation to ban distracted walking.[59] The survey asked 1,013 people if they would support legislation that would ban the use of hand-held cellphones while crossing a street. The survey was broken down by age and gender and found both men and women favoured a ban. Adults over 35 were most in favour, but even 51% of those aged 18-34 said they would support a ban on distracted walking.

Believe it or not a city in China has actually created a "phone lane" for texting pedestrians. Perhaps there needs to be an app that alerts pedestrians when they are about to crash into something. Unfortunately there is no app of that kind; instead there are augmented reality apps that are causing users to be even more glued to their smartphone screens, blurring the line between the real world and the virtual world. The "Pokémon Go" app became wildly

56. Ohio State (2013, June 13) *Distracted Walking: Injuries Soar for Pedestrians on Phones, Cell Phone Use Not Just Dangerous for Drivers, Study Finds* Retrieved from: http://researchnews.osu.edu/archive/distractwalk.htm

57. Carol M. Ostrom, C. (2012, Dec. 12) Seattle Times. *Dangerous distraction: Study finds many texting pedestrians* Retrieved from: http://www.seattletimes.com/seattle-news/dangerous-distraction-study-finds-many-texting-pedestrians/

58. Thompson, L., Rivara, F., Ayyagari, R., Ebel, B. (Dec. 2012) *Impact of social and technological distraction on pedestrian crossing behaviour: an observational study.* Retrieved from: http://injuryprevention.bmj.com/content/early/2012/12/06/injuryprev-2012-040601.abstract

59. Yeung, L. CBC News (Oct 27, 2016) *Majority of Canadians support legislation to ban distracted walking, poll suggests.* Retrieved from: http://www.cbc.ca/news/canada/british-columbia/majority-of-canadians-support-legislation-to-ban-distracted-walking-poll-suggests-1.3822086

popular immediately after its release in 2016.[60] The app uses your smartphone camera and GPS to create a game where you physically chase after and catch Pokémon characters that are superimposed on your smartphone screen at real world locations. There have been many reports of minor injuries due to people not paying attention to their surroundings while playing the game. There are concerns about users seriously injuring themselves or putting themselves in danger by being lured to secluded locations. It's strongly recommended that participants be aware of their surroundings at all times, travel in groups and never play while driving.

Your Body is Telling You Something

Scott Griessel@123RF.com   Sebastian Kaulitzki@123RF.com

There are other injuries causing concern when it comes to social media use, including thumb, wrist and forearm strain. Repetitive texting could cause inflammation of the tendons causing cramping or numbness in the fingers, wrist and forearm. It is sometimes referred to as "Text Claw,"

60. Nakashima, R. (2016, July 9) The Associated Press, CTV News. *New 'Pokemon Go' smartphone game leading to real-world injuries*. Retrieved from: http://www.ctvnews.ca/entertainment/new-pokemon-go-smartphone-game-leading-to-real-world-injuries-1.2979953

which could lead to tendonitis.[61] Holding a cell phone to your ear repeatedly for too long can cause what's referred to as "cell phone elbow," which is damage to an essential nerve in the arm caused by bending the elbow too tightly for a prolonged period of time.[62] It stretches and chokes the blood supply to the nerves. People who have this condition, which is technically called cubital tunnel syndrome, can feel tingling in the ring and pinky finger and weakness in the hands. If you experience these symptoms experts recommend switching hands periodically before it gets worse and causes further issues.

Another term called "Computer Vision Syndrome" is causing digital eye strain.[63] The American Optometric Association describes Computer Vision Syndrome as "a group of eye and vision-related problems that result from prolonged computer, tablet, e-reader and cell phone use." Optometrists are noticing more kids are being diagnosed with nearsightedness and they are blaming increased screen time. A study from the UK tracked more than 1000 children over six years, and compared results from similar studies in the 1960s.

They discovered that the number of children with myopia (the medical term for nearsightedness) has skyrocketed in the last five decades. Along with increased screen time, experts also believe it's because of lack of natural daylight. The researchers conclude that children are twice as likely

61. Bachai, S. (2014, Mar.31.) Medical Daily. *What is Text Claw?* Retrieved from: http://www.medicaldaily.com/what-text-claw-and-why-its-not-same-carpal-tunnel-syndrome-yet-273564

62. Park, M. (2009, June 2) *More talking, more problems: 'Cell phone elbow' damages nerves* CNN, Retrieved from: http://www.cnn.com/2009/HEALTH/06/02/cell.phone.elbow/index.html?iref=24hours

63. American Optometric Association. *Computer Vision Syndrome.* Retrieved from: *http://www.aoa.org/patients-and-public/caring-for-your-vision/protecting-your-vision/computer-vision-syndrome?sso=y*

to be nearsighted today than fifty years ago.[64] Experts say that spending just an extra hour a day in the sunshine each day should improve children's eyesight. They also recommend the 20-20-20 rule to prevent digital eye strain. Every 20 minutes look ahead and focus on an object 20 feet away for at least 20 seconds.

Another term used to describe neck and back strain from social media is "Text Neck." Dr. Dean Fishman, a chiropractor in Florida coined the term Text Neck when he noticed more and more young people were coming in complaining of neck pain, headaches, shoulder pain, or numbness and tingling into the upper extremity.[65] He noticed something unusual and common in all their x-rays; signs of premature spinal degeneration, a degeneration most often seen in middle-aged people who had spent several decades of their life with poor posture.

He theorized that prolonged periods of tilting the head downward to peer into a mobile device creates excessive strain on the cervical spine, causing spinal degeneration. Looking down and dropping your head forward changes the natural curvature of your neck. Over time that misalignment can strain muscles and cause wear and tear on the structures of the neck. Neck muscles, in their proper position, are designed to support the weight of your head, about 10 to 12 pounds. According to research on pain management by Dr. Robert Bolash from Cleveland; for every inch you drop your head forward, you double the load on

64. Spencer, B. (2016, Jan. 20) *Children are twice as likely to be short-sighted than 50 Years Ago.* Daily Mail. Retrieved from: http://www.dailymail.co.uk/health/article-3408587/Children-TWICE-likely-short-sighted-50-years-ago-Experts-blame-screen-time-lack-daylight.html

65. Fishman, D. (2015). *TEXT NECK® is a Global Epidemic.* Retrieved from: http://text-neck.com/

your neck muscles. Looking down at your smartphone with your chin to your chest can put up to 60 pounds of force on your neck.[66]

It Breaks Down Like This:

- 0 degrees-10-12 pounds (normal)
- 15 degrees-27 pounds of force
- 30 degrees-40 pounds of force
- 45 degrees-45 pounds of force
- 60 degrees-60 pounds of force

Tips to Avoid "Text Neck"

1. Straighten Up

Learn proper posture and neck alignment by peeking at your profile in a mirror. If you're standing correctly, you should be able to draw a vertical line from your ear to your shoulder.

2. Arch Back

Arch your neck and upper back backward, pulling your shoulders into alignment under your ears.

3. Look Forward

Raise the device to eye level. The same goes for your desktop computer. Your monitor screen should be at eye level so your head isn't perpetually dropping and causing muscle strain.

---

66. Bolash, R. (2015). *Text Neck: Is Smartphone Use Causing Your Neck Pain?* Retrieved from Cleveland Clinic website: https://health.clevelandclinic.org/2015/03/text-neck-is-smartphone-use-causing-your-neck-pain/

CHAPTER EIGHT

Internet Addiction

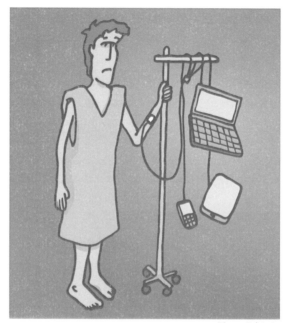

Diego Schtutman@123RF.com

Dictionary.com defines addiction as "the state of being enslaved to a habit or practice or to something that is psychologically or physically habit-forming." Merriam-Webster defines addiction as "a strong and harmful need to regularly have something or do something." There is an addictive need to be connected 24/7 with a cell phone, tablet or computer always within reach, mostly because of FOMO (fear of missing out). Many people are addicted to the internet because they crave the constant stimulation it provides. A 2013 study of Internet users, published online in the international journal PLOS ONE, found that heavy Internet users can suffer withdrawal symptoms similar to substance abusers.[67] Professor Phil Reed, who reported the results of the study, says "when these people come off-line, they suffer increased negative mood – just like people coming off illegal drugs like ecstasy." We have become addicted to taking a scroll through the virtual world from first thing in the morning to last thing at night. Like any other addiction, it's vital to recognize it and take steps to break the addiction.

Tips to Break Social Media Addiction

No Devices at the Dinner Table

Dinner time should be family time. Family meals can create feelings of closeness, security and overall comfort. Researchers note that children tend to communicate more at the dinner table allowing parents a good opportunity to connect with their children. So turn off any distractions like the TV and all cell phones. This will allow for all family members to share and connect.

Pledge to Take a Tech "Time Out"

It's important to balance the virtual world with the real world, and to recognize what you may be missing out on by always being connected. There is so much more to benefit from in the real world — exploring nature, exercise, fun

---

67. Reed, P., Osborne, L., Truzoli, R., Romano, M. Swansea University (2013) *Study finds 'Internet addicts' can suffer similar withdrawal symptoms to substance mis-users.* Retrieved from: http://www.swansea.ac.uk/mediacentre/newsarchive/2013/studyfindsinternetaddictscansuffersimilar-withdrawalsymptomstosubstancemis-users.php

and games, sports, playgrounds, swimming pools, visiting and so much more. Many kids today haven't experienced unstructured free play, and the only games they're familiar with are online games. The biggest challenge with taking a tech time out is trying to rip the phone out of their hands, but many young people have admitted that they actually enjoyed taking a tech time out. Getting over the first hurdle is always the hardest. Unplug from technology and plug into the real world from time to time.

No Devices When Out for Dinner

How many times have you seen it, a family out for dinner and they are all on their phones. Some restaurants actually provide tablets for kids instead of crayons. We already covered this earlier. The word is "Phubbing." Don't be a "Phubber."

No Devices at Bed Time

More on this later

Balance Online Activity with Face to Face Interaction

We have covered the importance of face to face communication. True connection with someone happens in person.

Alter Your Settings

Do you really need to have your phone alert you for every text, email or news feed? It distracts you from you being able to enjoy the moment and the people you are with. It's also annoying for people around you. It's a noisy enough world — let's try to do our part to reduce noise pollution.

Check with a Purpose

We have covered the importance of asking yourself what is motivating me to go online? Have a legitimate reason for going online. Don't just check out of boredom. That message, news feed or cat video will still be there later.

Set a Time Limit

Have you noticed that time can just slip away when you are on social media? It can really grab your attention and keep you scrolling along for hours on end. Setting a time limit allows you to have control over it.

Identify Emotions that are Causing You to Gravitate Towards Social Media

Again we have covered this. If you are feeling down and you are looking for acceptance or experiencing low self-esteem, the virtual world will only make it worse. Identify any triggers that cause you to gravitate towards social media. Stay in the real world and talk to a friend, family member or your healthcare provider.

Take Control of Social Media

Social media can be addictive and like any other addiction it can control you. You have to take control of it.

Video Game Addiction

Oleg Dudko@123rf.com

Everyone would agree that video games are fun to play. Even if you haven't played lately, you most likely played at some time in your life. The 2016 Entertainment Software Association annual report on gaming habits in America was released in 2016. The survey of over 4,000 households nationwide found that 63% of U.S. households surveyed include at least one frequent gamer. 47% of gamers are between 18 and 49 years old. The average man who plays games is 35; the average woman is 44. The survey also revealed 59% of those who play games on a regular basis are men and 41% are women.[68]

Commercial video games have been around since the early 1970's. Early video games were large and freestanding and played in video arcades. The first successful commercial arcade game was introduced by Atari in 1972. The

68. Entertainment Software Association. (2016) Retrieved from: http://essentialfacts.theesa.com/Essential-Facts-2016.pdf

game was called Pong, and was an instant hit when it was released. Pong used two dimensional graphics to simulate a table tennis game. The player or players would control an on screen paddle by moving it vertically across the side of the screen; players use the paddles to hit a tiny square shape back and forth across the screen. The game speeds up as you progress. Points are earned when one person fails to return the square to the other player. In 1975, Atari introduced a home version of its popular arcade game. Other popular early (now considered classic) video games include Asteroids, Tetris, Space Invaders, Frogger, Super Mario Bros., Donkey Kong and Pac-Man, just to name a few.

Video games today have greatly evolved due to the advancement of technology. You no longer have to go to an arcade to play. Gamers can play 24/7 anywhere on dedicated systems such as PlayStation or Nintendo Wii, personal or tablet computers or cell phones. Graphics are much more advanced, enhancing the gaming experience with near life-like images. When playing older video games, it was obvious that you were suspending reality to play, but the lifelike images today can blur the line between the real world and the virtual world. Some of the most popular video games today include Grand Theft Auto, Call of Duty and Halo. All have become controversial for their violent content. Many of the top selling video games today contain extreme graphic violence.

As the level of violence in video games has increased, so has the concern about the effect on the players. There has been much discussion over the years on whether aggressive and violent behaviour is a result of violence in video games, or that those who play already have aggressive and violent tendencies which draw them to violent games. There is strong support on both sides of the argument. One main concern about violent video games is that gaming is not passive; you are an active participant in the game. Unlike television, where you watch violent acts, video games have you commit the violent acts, which experts warn could affect your thought patterns. The game allows you to be rewarded for violent acts rather than punished, and if played enough could skew a person's view on violence and its consequences. It could also lead to desensitizing gamers to violent acts and behaviors. Long-term effects of violent video games have not been clinically documented, but it is recommended that parents closely monitor the amount of time their kids spend playing video games and be aware of any negative effects.

Can something that is meant to be enjoyable and fun become addictive and destructive to your life? Playing the occasional video game for fun is typically harmless. There can be benefits including improved hand-eye coordination and decision making skills, boost self-confidence, creativity and even provide education. There have been studies documenting the benefits of playing video games, especially as children grow and develop. Researchers claim games allow children to test out different social scenarios and learn how to handle the kinds of conflicts they might face in the real world. They say it allows children to develop an understanding of how to deal with power, dominance, aggression, pain, and separation, practiced in non-threatening conditions.[69] Unfortunately, many people use video games to escape reality which could lead to addiction.

Many believe that video game addiction is real and a major problem in society. Unlike older video games where players were forced to start over after losing, modern day video games are open-ended, allowing players to save their place and pick back up again to keep levelling up in the game; this can cause players to mull over and ponder their next move in a game while involved in other activities. Video game designers want more people to play their video games so they make them just challenging enough to keep you coming back for more but not so hard that you eventually give up.

There are two common types of video games and therefore two types of video game addiction. One type is generally designed to be played by a single player with one clear goal or mission. The addiction is often related to completing the mission or beating a high score. Another type of video game involves multiple players playing together online; it's called MMORPG or massively multiplayer online role-playing game. The addiction can come from escaping reality and connection with a community where gamers feel the most accepted.

In the medical world, addiction is commonly associated with the abuse of alcohol, drugs, smoking, sex, pornography and gambling. The American Academy of Child and Adolescent Psychiatry spokesman Dr. Michael Brody says in order to be considered an addict, a person must have created a strong

---

69. Vitelli, R. Psychology Today (Feb. 2014) *Are There Benefits in Playing Video Games? What are the positive benefits of playing video games?* Retrieved from: https://www.psychologytoday.com/blog/media-spotlight/201402/are-there-benefits-in-playing-video-games

dependence on a substance or behavior and the failure to obtain or participate in it causes irritability and unhappiness. Video game addiction is described as an impulse control disorder which is very similar to pathological gambling. According to psychiatrist Michael Brody, MD, the criteria for video game addiction is the same as that for addiction to a substance. The person craves and requires the source to the point of becoming irritable when they cannot access it, and will experience withdrawal symptoms and are likely to exhibit anger, violence and depression.[70] "It affects the same pleasure centers in the brain that make people want to come back," says Dr. Michael Fraser, a clinical psychologist and professor at Weill Cornell Medical College in New York.

According to studies from the University of New Mexico, up to 15 percent of all gamers exhibit signs that could be characterized as addiction.[71][72] Statistics show that men and boys are more likely to become addicted to video games versus women and girls. Recent research has found that nearly one in 10 youth gamers (ages 8-18) can be classified as pathological gamers or addicted to video-gaming.[73] In 2016, following nearly two decades of research, the American Psychiatric Association officially recognized Internet Gaming Disorder as a condition that requires consideration by clinicians and researchers. Internet Gaming Disorder appeared in the updated version of the *Diagnostic*

70. Psychguides.com. (2016) *Video Game Addiction Symptoms, Causes and Effects*. Retrieved from: http://www.psychguides.com/guides/video-game-addiction-symptoms-causes-and-effects/

71. Psychguides.com. (2016) *Video Game Addiction Symptoms, Causes and Effects*. Retrieved from: http://www.psychguides.com/guides/video-game-addiction-symptoms-causes-and-effects/

72. Ashwoodrecovery.com (2016) *The Real Story About Video Game Addiction*. Retrieved from: https://ashwoodrecovery.com/blog/video-game-addiction/

73. Unity Point Health, Illinois Institute for Addiction Recovery (2016) *What is Video-game addiction?* Retrieved from: http://www.addictionrecov.org/Addictions/?AID=45

and Statistical Manual for Mental Disorders (DSM-5) for the first time, recommending additional clinical research and study to recognize Internet Gaming Disorder as a formal disorder.[74]

How to Recognize Video Game Addiction

Like any other addiction, video game addiction has warning signs. Though the addiction can have significant consequences to those suffering from it, the warning signs can sometimes be very difficult to recognize.

It is important to know how to recognize these signs for yourself or someone you care about. According to the Illinois Institute for Addiction Recovery, symptoms can be both emotional and physical.[75]

Warning Signs

- Playing for 24-30 hours a week
- Playing in secret
- Lying to friends and family regarding the amount of time spent playing
- Mulling over video games when engrossed in other activities
- Sacrificing time at work or school in order to play
- Using games to escape from reality
- Isolation from others in order to spend more time gaming
- Becoming alienated from friends and family

74. dsm5.org. (2016) Internet Gaming Disorder. Retrieved from: http://www.dsm5.org/Documents/Internet%20Gaming%20Disorder%20Fact%20Sheet.pdf

75. Psychguides.com. (2016) *Video Game Addiction Symptoms, Causes and Effects* Retrieved from: http://www.psychguides.com/guides/video-game-addiction-symptoms-causes-and-effects/

- Becoming irritated if unable to play
- Lacking enough hours of sleep
- Losing interest in other activities and hobbies
- Increasingly ignoring personal hygiene

Emotional Symptoms of Video Game Addiction May Include:

- Feelings of restlessness, moodiness and/or irritability when unable to play
- Preoccupation with thoughts of previous online activity or anticipation of the next online session
- Anxiety and/or depression

Physical Symptoms of Video Game Addiction May Include:

- Fatigue
- Migraines due to intense concentration or eye strain
- Dry or red eyes
- Carpal tunnel syndrome caused by the overuse of a controller or computer mouse
- Poor physical health or weight gain

Video Game Addiction and Depression

There have been lots of theories over the years about whether there is a link between video game addiction and mental health issues. Two studies of gamers followed large groups of teenagers over a one and two year period time to assess how much time they spend playing video games and to monitor their mental health over the study period.

The first study published in the journal Pediatrics in 2011 followed 3,000 students in grades 3, 4, 7 and 8 from Singapore.[76] After two years the study found that children who were more impulsive and less comfortable with other children spent more time playing video games; an average of 31 hours a week. The study also concluded that they were more likely to suffer from depression, anxiety and social phobias than those who played video games less often. They were also more likely to see a drop in their school grades and experience relationship issues with their parents.[77] In the study, some gamers who decreased their playing time showed fewer symptoms of depression.

Another study released in 2010 published in The Archives of Pediatric and Adolescent Medicine followed more than 1,000 Chinese teenagers ages 13 to 18.[78] [79] After nine

76. Gentile, D., Choo, H., Liau,A., Li,T., Fung, D. Khoo, A., AAP News and Journals Gateway (Jan. 2011) *Pathological Video Game Use Among Youths: A Two-Year Longitudinal Study.* Retrieved from: http://pediatrics.aappublications.org/content/early/2011/01/17/peds.2010-1353.abstract

77. Rabin, R. The New York Times. nytimes.com. (Jan. 2011) *Video Games and the Depressed Teenager.* Retrieved from: http://well.blogs.nytimes.com/2011/01/18/video-games-and-the-depressed-teenager/?_r=3

78. Rabin, R. The New York Times. nytimes.com. (Jan. 2011) *Video Games and the Depressed Teenager.* Retrieved from: http://well.blogs.nytimes.com/2011/01/18/video-games-and-the-depressed-teenager/?_r=3

79. Lam, L., Peng, Z. The Jama Network. (Aug. 2010) *Effect of Pathological Use of the Internet on Adolescent Mental Health.* Retrieved from: http://jamanetwork.com/journals/jamapediatrics/article-abstract/383813

months the study concluded that those who played video games excessively were more than twice as likely as others to be depressed.

Not everyone is convinced by the studies that video game addiction causes depression. Dr. Douglas Gentile, an associate professor of psychology at Iowa State University, says a range of mental health problems in youth combined with "pathological gaming" may develop in tandem; much like the flu and pneumonia which can feed off one another and lead to new problems. He says "You can get the flu, and then get pneumonia, which is a different thing, but it kind of came along with the flu, and flu made you at greater risk for it, and then, once you got the pneumonia, you're at risk from something else." Dr. Gentile says that teenagers who are experiencing mental health issues may retreat into video gaming, which could increase symptoms. He suggests parents regulate their children's use of video games and trust their instincts on what constitutes excessive use.

No expert would ever recommend avoiding playing video games all together, but most would recommend using common sense and monitor time spent playing video games as well as identify any negative effects on your life.

Tips to Break Video Game Addiction[80]

- Make gaming a weekend activity, or limit your "screen time" to an hour a night.
- Stay active in hobbies you've always enjoyed, or try a new sport, volunteer activity or extracurricular pursuit.
- Make real-life relationships a priority. Even though the virtual fantasy world can be enticing, schedule time with friends, family and loved ones regularly.

According to Dr. Michael Fraser in a New York Daily News article, kids, adolescents and teens often resort to playing video games to try to resolve any mental health issues. He says video game and internet addiction usually point to other mental problems including anxiety, depression and trouble forming healthy relationships.[81] He recommends parents help their children learn how to overcome problems in real life rather than giving up and allowing them to rely on fantasies in games.

Parents should implement a reasonable schedule for when playing games are allowed. Alternatively, you can just replace gaming with another pastime that would be equally as stimulating. You can also use playing games as a reward whenever your child successfully resolves personal problems in real life.

Like any other addiction, it's important to recognize the addiction and be totally honest with yourself and others.

80. Video Game Addiction. *When video games become more than just games.* (2016) Retrieved from: http://www.video-game-addiction.org/

81. Miller, T. New York Daily News ((Mar. 2013) *Video game addiction and other Internet compulsive disorders mask depression, anxiety, learning disabilities.* Retrieved from: http://www.ny-dailynews.com/life-style/health/kids-addicted-video-games-violent-experts-article-1.1298338

Gaming addiction can result in personal, family, academic, financial, occupational and mental health problems. If video games are impairing your daily life and damaging personal relationships, causing work or school problems and feelings of anxiety and depression, it may be time to seek help. There are specific 12-step programs and addiction centres designed for internet and video game addiction. Talk to an addiction counsellor as soon as possible before the addiction affects all areas of your life. As alluring as the virtual world can be, it's important for your mental health to take frequent tech time-outs to reconnect with nature, family and friends, and discover self-care activities that do not include screen time. Only the real world can meet your emotional and social needs.

Children and Technology: How Young is Too Young?

Leung Cho Pan@123RF.com   Benjamin Harben@123RF.com

You don't have to look very far to see someone on a handheld device. But you may be surprised to see children as young as 1 or 2 years old swiping on a tablet. Young children are exposed to mobile devices because most parents have them, and children are attracted to the devices. Many restaurants are now offering tablets to their very young guests. A study of 370 parents done by Dr. Hilda Kabali, a pediatric resident at Einstein Medical Center in Philadelphia, shows that by age 1, more than one-third of their babies had touched or scrolled the screen of a mobile device. By age 2, more than half had watched a TV show on the device, played video games or used an app, and more than one quarter were using mobile devices for at least an hour a day.[82]

The American Academy of Pediatrics and the Canadian Pediatric Society state infants aged 0-2 years should not have any exposure to technology, 3-5 years be restricted to one hour per day, and 6-18 years restricted to two hours per day.[83] [84]

There are many who believe that exposing children to technology at a young age, in moderation, has its benefits, mostly due to early learning apps. But there are also those who believe no child under the age of 12 should be exposed to technology. Pediatric occupational therapist and child development expert Cris Rowan is an outspoken critic on the impact of technology on human development, behavior, and productivity. She believes technology is eroding children's foundations for development and learning, and is calling on parents,

82. Haelle, T. (2015, Apr. 26). *Very Young Kids Often Use Tablets, Smartphones, Study Finds.* Health Day. Retrieved from: https://consumer.healthday.com/caregiving-information-6/infant-and-child-care-health-news-410/very-young-kids-often-use-tablets-smartphones-study-finds-698762.html

83. Brown, A., Shifrin, D., Hill, D. (2015, Oct.) *Beyond turn it off: How to advise families on media use.* American Academy of Pediatrics. Retrieved from: http://www.aappublications.org/content/36/10/54

84. Canadian Pediatric Society (2016). *Tips for limiting screen time at home.* Retrieved from http://www.caringforkids.cps.ca/handouts/limiting_screen_time_at_home

teachers and governments to ban the use of all handheld devices for children under the age of 12 years.[85] [86]

She cites research-based reasons for calling for the ban. This research looked at how technology use could impact early brain development, contribute to obesity, sleep deprivation, addictions, aggression, and mental illness.

85. Rowan, C. (2016) *A research review regarding the impact of technology on child development, behavior, and academic performance.* Retrieved from: http://www.sd23.bc.ca/ProgramsServices/earlylearning/parentinformation/Documents/Impact%20of%20Technology%20on%20Young%20Children's%20Development.pdf

86. Rowan, C. (2015, March 3) *10 Reasons Why Handheld Devices Should Be Banned for Children Under the Age of 12.* [Blog post].Retrieved from Huffington Post website: http://www.huffingtonpost.com/cris-rowan/10-reasons-why-handheld-devices-should-be-banned_b_4899218.html

Chapter Nine

Screen Time and Bedtime

Aleksandr Khakimullin@123RF.com   Vitaliy Vodolazskyy@123RF.com

Sleep plays a vital role in good mental and physical health and well-being throughout your life. Getting enough quality sleep at the right times can help protect your mental health, physical health, quality of life and safety. The way you feel while you're awake greatly depends on what happens while you're sleeping.

Benefits of a Good Night's Sleep

- Improves memory
- Sharpens attention
- Lowers stress
- Spurs creativity
- Curbs inflammation
- Helps maintain a healthy weight

- Improves overall physical health
- Less likely to get ill
- Helps anxiety and depression symptoms
- Look more attractive
- Possibly live longer

Chronic Sleep Deprivation Effects

- Obesity
- Diabetes
- Hypertension
- Low immune system
- Cardiovascular problems
- Impaired memory and academic/work performance
- Aggressive or inappropriate behavior
- Increased risk of anxiety and depression

It's estimated 60–70% of Canadian students arriving at school are extremely fatigued (2011 Douglas Mental Health University Institute).[87]

According to the Pew Research Centre (2010) and Stanford University (2013), 70–84% of youth sleep with their cell phones next to them on a nightstand or under their pillow just in case they get a text or call during the night.[88] [89]

87. Gruber, R. (2016). *60-70% of Canadian students are shown to be extremely fatigued when they arrive at school*. Retrieved from Douglas Mental Health University Institute website: http://www.douglas.qc.ca/info/sleep-and-children-impact-of-lack-of-sleep-on-daily-life

88. Lenhart, A. (2010, Sept.) *Part Four: A comparison of cell phone attitudes & use between teens and adults*. Pew Research Centre. Retrieved from: http://www.pewinternet.org/2010/09/02/part-four-a-comparison-of-cell-phone-attitudes-use-between-teens-and-adults/

89. Smith, J. (2013) Sept. 10) *Recommendation: Do Not Sleep With Your Smartphone*. Retrieved from: http://www.hostdime.com/blog/do-not-sleep-with-your-smartphone/

Even 20% of grade 4 students said they sleep with their cell phones (Media Smarts 2014).[90]

Screen Time Facts

Studies show that screen time before bedtime can significantly affect both quantity and quality of sleep. It has been proven that exposure to light from computer tablets significantly lowers levels of the hormone melatonin, which plays a role in the sleep cycle regulating our biological clocks.

Melatonin is secreted by the pineal gland especially in response to darkness, and regulates our circadian rhythm, a 24-hour cycle that tells our bodies when to sleep. Researchers say melatonin suppression may not only cause sleep disturbances, but also raise the risk of obesity, diabetes and other disorders.

Screen Time Recommendations

Experts recommend avoiding all screen time 1-2 hours before bed.[91] That includes TV, computer, and all handheld devices. They also recommend no devices in the bedroom. It's imperative that everyone in the household follow these recommendations. You need to be aware of the possible effects of chronic sleep deprivation and the benefits of a good night's sleep. Parents need to challenge themselves and their children to identify self-care activities that can replace screen time before bed. Examples could include:

90. Media Smarts. (2014) *Young Canadians in a wired world Phase III*. Retrieved from: http://mediasmarts.ca/sites/mediasmarts/files/pdfs/publication-report/full/YCWWIII_Life_Online_FullReport.pdf
91. Keep Safe. *No Screen Time Before Bed*. Retrieved from: http://ikeepsafe.org/be-a-pro/balance/no-screen-time-before-bed/

read a book, play with the dog, listen to music, journal, have a bubble bath, do arts and crafts, play a game, or anything else that does not include screen time. When everyone starts to experience the benefits of a tech time out, especially before bed, it may encourage more tech time outs which will continue to benefit the mental and physical health of all family members.

Sleeping Pill and Melatonin Supplement Use

The number of prescriptions for sleeping pills has skyrocketed in North America. The number of prescriptions dispensed in Canada rose from 16.4 million in 2006 to more than 20 million in 2011, according to market research firm IMS Brogan.[92] The Centers for Disease Control and Prevention study of 17,000 adults from 2005 through 2010 revealed 9 million people in the United States use prescription sleeping pills.[93]

Most prescription sleep aids are intended for short-term use, but many are using them long-term. Experts are concerned that long-term use of sleep aids could cause addiction and serious side effects. In our fast-paced society, instead of looking at what may be causing insomnia (chronic stress, mental health issues, screen time), people look for a "quick fix" to the problem.

---

92. Kirkey, S. (2012,July 12) *The big sleep: Canada's dangerous love affair with tranquillizers.* Post Media News. Retrived from: http://www.canada.com/health/sleep+Canada+dangerous+love+aff air+with+tranquillizers/6924323/story.html

93. NY Daily News/Associated Press (2013, Aug 30) *CDC: 9 million Americans use prescription sleeping pills.* Retrieved from: http://www.nydailynews.com/life-style/health/cdc-9-million-americans-sleeping-pills-article-1.1441778

Doctors and researchers are reporting an increasing number of parents are giving a melatonin supplement to their children to help them fall asleep, despite concerns about the potential impact of the supplement on children's health, particularly long term. Sales of the melatonin supplement, a synthetic form of the naturally occurring hormone, have increased more than 500 percent in the U.S since 2003 — from $62 million to $378 million in 2014, according to the Nutrition Business Journal.[94] In a 2013 Globe and Mail article, doctors warn parents about the risks of giving their children melatonin supplements.[95] Their main concerns are that the supplement is not regulated and the effects on a child's development are largely unknown. "The long-term safety data is simply not there," says Dr. Mark Feldman, director of community pediatrics at the University of Toronto. Since the hormone is considered a dietary supplement similar to vitamins or minerals, synthetic melatonin is not controlled or regulated like other pharmaceutical drugs, and is available without a prescription in Canada and the U.S.

Health Canada classifies melatonin as a natural health product that is used to treat sleep disorders in adults, and is available over the counter in many forms, including capsules, chewables (e.g. gummies, tablets), liquids, powders, and flavoured strips. It's important to note that melatonin is only available with a prescription in many European countries as well as Australia.

94. Schroeder M. (2015, October 6) *More Parents Are Giving Kids Melatonin to Sleep. Is It Safe?* Retrieved from US News web site: http://health.usnews.com/health-news/patient-advice/articles/2015/10/06/more-parents-are-giving-kids-melatonin-to-sleep-is-it-safe

95. Eastwood, J. (2013, July 9). *If I send my kid to bed with melatonin, will it hurt him?* Globe and Mail. Retrieved from http://www.theglobeandmail.com/life/health-and-fitness/if-i-send-my-kid-to-bed-with-melatonin-will-it-hurt-him/article13100349/

In early 2015, sleep researchers at the University of Adelaide in Australia warned doctors and parents *not* to give melatonin to kids to help them sleep. In a paper published in the Journal of Pediatrics and Child Health, authored by Professor David Kennaway, he cautioned that giving kids a melatonin supplement may result in serious side effects when the children are older.[96] Dr. Shelly Weiss, a neurologist at the Hospital for Sick Children in Toronto says since melatonin is a hormone, it could delay a child's development during puberty.[97]

To date, there are no long term research studies that have definitively determined whether there is a downside to children taking melatonin. Because of limited data about any side effects associated with the use of melatonin in the pediatric population, Health Canada is encouraging parents and caregivers to consult a healthcare professional before giving any natural health products containing melatonin to children. Whether safe or not, experts stress that it's important for parents to first seek to understand and address the root cause of sleep problems rather than reach for a quick fix. There is a risk that the child will come to rely on the melatonin supplement to fall asleep, rather than learn good sleep hygiene, which is defined as: a variety of different practices that are necessary to have normal, quality nighttime sleep and full daytime alertness. It's important for all ages to develop good sleep hygiene.

96. Kennaway, D. J. (2015, Feb. 25) *Potential safety issues in the use of the hormone melatonin in pediatrics.* https://www.adelaide.edu.au/news/news76502.html

97. CBC News (2013, July 7). *Melatonin no 'magic pill' for getting healthy kids to sleep. CBC News.* Retrieved from http://www.cbc.ca/news/health/melatonin-no-magic-pill-for-getting-healthy-kids-to-sleep-1.1328368

Healthy Sleep Tips

Stick to a Sleep Schedule

Have the same bedtime and wake up time, even on the weekends. This helps to regulate your body's clock and could help you fall asleep and stay asleep for the night.

Exercise Daily

Vigorous exercise is best, but even light exercise is better than no activity. No exercise immediately before bed.

Evaluate Your Room

Design your sleep environment to establish the conditions you need for sleep. Your bedroom should be cool — between 60 and 67 degrees. Your bedroom should be free from any noise (except white noise) that can disturb your sleep. Finally, your bedroom should be free from any light.

Sleep On a Comfortable Mattress and Pillow

Choose the mattress and pillow that provides the correct comfort and support.

Avoid Alcohol, Cigarettes, and Heavy Meals in the Evening

Alcohol, cigarettes and caffeine can disrupt sleep. Eating big or spicy meals can cause discomfort from indigestion that can make it hard to sleep. Avoid eating large meals for two to three hours before bedtime.

Choose a Relaxing Bedtime Routine

For example: have a bath and a hot milky drink before bed, read a book, listen to music, journal, meditate, etc. If you can't sleep, go into another room and do something relaxing until you feel tired.

If you're still having trouble sleeping, don't hesitate to speak with your doctor or find a sleep professional.

The National Sleep Foundation provides good information on the importance of sleep. NSF is the trusted resource for sleep science, healthy sleep habits and sleep disorders to medical professionals, patients and the public. Their website is **www.sleepfoundation.org**.

CHAPTER TEN

Practicing Online Safety

Gunnar Pippel@123RF.com

Remember that everything on the internet is traceable and leaves a "digital footprint." According to Webopedia, a digital footprint is used to describe "the trail, traces or "footprints" that people leave online." This is information transmitted online, such as forum registration, e-mails and attachments, uploading videos or digital images and any other form of transmission of information, all of which leaves traces of personal information about yourself available to others online.

Social Media Safety Tips

Keep Your Online Personal Identity Secret

General rule: Don't give out any information that someone could possibly use to steal your identity or to find you. Even "small clues" like what school you attend or the name of your sports team is enough for a predator to figure out your identity.

Don't Do Anything Online that You Wouldn't Do Offline

Sometimes people think they can get away with online behavior, but what you do in the virtual world is a reflection of who you are in the real world.

Don't "Friend" Strangers

Even though it feels good to add to your "Friend" total, if you really don't know them, don't accept the request. Even if they have a slight connection to you — they go to the same school, or they are a friend of your cousin, thoroughly check it out before accepting any request.

Never agree to meet someone in person that you only "met" online. People can pretend to be someone else online. You're probably aware of tragic events that have happened to young people who met someone in person that they only "met" online.

Check Your Privacy Settings

Ensure your privacy settings are set to what you want them to be.

Don't Give Out Your Passwords to Anyone (Except Parents)

You wouldn't give out your pin number for your debit card to just anyone. Don't let just anyone access your online accounts.

Think Twice Before Hitting "Enter" or "Send"

What you post is permanent and can't be taken back. Stop and think before sending anything. You may regret it later. As mentioned earlier, before hitting send follow the "WWGT" rule: What Would Grandma think?

Be Cautious About Posting Personal Photos Online

Be aware that photos could be used without permission for just about anything anywhere in the world. One family discovered that their annual holiday photo was being used as a storefront sign in the Czech Republic. In another story, a teenage girl discovered that her photo was being used as an advertisement for a wireless communications company halfway around the world. The picture you post today could also affect future job opportunities. There are many who regret posting certain pictures of themselves once they realized that employers use social media to screen applicants.

The bottom line is use common sense and think safety first. The rules about safety in the real world are the same rules that apply in the virtual world.

Two recomended online resources are: **www.safekids.com** and **www.safetynetkids.org**

Social Media Apps Raising Safety Concerns

Many parents are unaware of some popular social media apps that youth are using today. Many allow users to send messages anonymously, leading to new challenges for parents and law enforcement.

Ask.fm is a question and answer based social networking site used by millions of teens. This app allows users to interact in a question and answer format anonymously. The app is rated ages 13+ and is most popular in Europe, but is catching on in the U.S. and Canada. Because of its anonymous format, some have used the app for cyberbullying which has been linked to a number of suicides between 2012 and 2013. The father of a teenage girl in Leicestershire, England, called for changes to the social networking site after his daughter took her own life following months of online bullying. He wants the controversial website to ban all anonymous posts to stop online bullies hiding their true identities.[98]

In response to the uproar in UK, Ask.fm now has a higher-profile button for reporting bullying and a pledge to respond

98. Gladdis, K. (2013, August 19). *Ask.fm owners shamed into installing prominent panic button after death of 14-year-old but her grieving father calls for an end to anonymous posts. The Daily Mail.* Retrieved from http://www.dailymail.co.uk/news/article-2397381/Ask-fm-prominent-panic-buttons-added-site-death-14-year-old-Hannah-Smith.html

within 24 hours. But many believe the changes have not gone far enough and are calling for the site to be shut down.

Whisper is an app that allows users to share secrets anonymously and receive anonymous replies. Rated ages 17+.

Kik Messenger, also known as Kik, is a Canadian based app founded in 2009. Its main appeal is privacy and anonymity. The app allows people to create a user name, which can be fictitious, and communicate with strangers anonymously. The app is rated ages 13+ and does not require a phone number. The anonymity of the app makes Kik appealing, and is becoming a major concern for law enforcement. There are many cases of men using Kik to solicit nude photos from underage girls. In 2016, two Virginia Tech freshmen were charged with the premeditated kidnapping and killing of a 13-year-old girl who, authorities say, communicated with her murderer online using Kik.[99]

Kik has cooperated with law enforcement and is taking a variety of steps, including sponsoring an annual conference on crimes against children and posting a law enforcement guide on its website devoted to fielding law enforcement requests to help prevent child exploitation. An online petition was created to shut down Kik or force Kik to verify identity and age of users.

Yik Yak is an app that acts like a local gossip bulletin board which targets college students who want to share campus news or happenings, party information or just vent concerns. Those using the app are able to see messages from users within a set radius. The app is rated ages 17+ but younger users

99. Stolberg, S. Perez-Pena, R. (2016, Feb. 5) *Wildly Popular App Kik Offers Teenagers, and Predators, Anonymity.* The New York Times. Retrieved from: http://www.nytimes.com/2016/02/06/us/social-media-apps-anonymous-kik-crime.html?_r=0

are easily getting their hands on the app. It's an anonymous social wall and doesn't require any personal information other than the user's location. Yik Yak has a bad reputation amongst schools due to threats made on the app, causing safety concerns and disruptions for the schools and local police. In 2014, a Massachusetts-area high school was evacuated twice after bomb threats were posted to Yik Yak.[100]

Charges were laid against eleven U.S. college students for threats posted to Yik Yak in relation to eight universities. In 2015, an Ottawa area school was in lockdown after a threat was posted to Yik Yak claiming there was a gun in a science lab. The school was in lockdown while authorities investigated. The threat turned out to be a false alarm, but the incident prompted the school board to put a ban on the app in that school district.[101]

Yik Yak has responded to concerns about young teens using the app by blocking the app from middle and high school locations. An online petition was created to shut down Yik Yak, accusing the app of facilitating hate speech and bullying.

After School is another location-based private message board app for schools allowing students to post anonymously. Like Yik Yak, it has also raised concerns due to online threats and cyberbullying. It's rated ages 17+.

After School has responded to the concerns by adding new features designed to guard against abuse.

100. Bogart, N. (2015, Dec. 10) *What is Yik Yak? The latest app to cause concern at Canadian schools.* Global News. Retrieved from: http://globalnews.ca/news/1785227/what-is-yik-yak-the-latest-app-to-cause-concern-at-canadian-schools/

101. CBC News. (2015, Jan. 20) *Yik Yak app: Why schools are concerned.* Retrieved from: http://www.cbc.ca/news/technology/yik-yak-app-why-schools-are-concerned-1.2920155

Snapchat is not an anonymous app, but it is still raising concerns. The app allows users to post photos and videos that get deleted up to 10 seconds after they're received. Some kids are using the app to send more explicit and racy photos because they believe the images can't be saved and circulated. But the truth is users can take a screenshot before an image is deleted in the app. It's rated ages 12+.

The truth is, the majority of apps are usually harmless and fun, but experts warn this new class of apps that offer anonymity pose significant risks for teenagers. These types of apps make it easier for users to conceal their identities to try to lure teens, spread pornography, threats and hate messages.

"Sharenting"
Are Parents Sharing Too Much About Their Kids on Social Media?

vectorshots@123RF.com   newartgraphics@123RF.com

You don't have to look very far on social media to find pictures or videos of young children that were posted by their parents. Kids who are too young to post on social media themselves have no control over what their parents post online, and some parents tend to overshare pictures of their kids. It is referred to as "Sharenting." It is the combination of the words sharing and parenting. Sharenting is when parents share *too much information* (TMI) about their children online. The term was first credited in a Wall Street Journal article by Steven Leckart where he refers to oversharing by parents on social media as "Oversharenting."

A national poll in 2014 from the C.S. Mott Children's Hospital at the University of Michigan found that more than half of mothers and one third of fathers share information about their children on social media.[102] [103]

Nearly 75% of parents say sharing on social media makes them feel less alone. According to the poll that surveyed a national sample of parents of children aged 0-4, the most common topics shared on social media included sleep, nutrition, discipline, daycare/preschool and behavior.

Nearly 70% of parents said they use social media to get advice from other parents and 62% said it helped them worry less. The question is how much is too much sharing? The poll showed that 27% shared inappropriate photos of a child, 51% gave information that could identify a child's location, and 56% gave embarrassing information about a child. Parents need to be cautious about sharing embarrassing information or photos of their children because the child may not appreciate it when they're older.

Parents in the poll did recognize potential risks of over-sharing. About 68% stated they were worried about their child's privacy and someone sharing the photo of the child, and more than 50% were worried that their child will be embarrassed when older. Sarah J. Clark, associate director of Mott Children's Hospital national poll and associate research scientist at the University of Michigan Department of Pediatrics says "by the time children are old enough to use social media themselves, many already have a digital

---

102. C.S. Mott Children's Hospital, University of Michigan Health System (2015, March 16). *"Sharenting" trends: Do parents share too much about their kids on social media?* Retrieved from: http://www.mottchildren.org/news/archive/201503/%E2%80%9Csharenting%E2%80%9D-trends-do-parents-share-too-much-about-their

103. C.S. Mott Children's Hospital, the University of Michigan Department of Pediatrics and Communicable Diseases, and the University of Michigan Child Health Evaluation and Research (CHEAR) Unit. (2015, March 16) *Parents on Social Media: Likes and Dislikes of Sharenting.* Retrieved from: http://mottnpch.org/sites/default/files/documents/031615_sharenting_0.pdf

identity created for them by their parents." She admits social networking sites bring parents together to share in ways that weren't possible before, "however, there's potential for the line between sharing and oversharing to get blurred."

Parents in France who post photos of their kids on social media without their permission could face fines of over $49,000 or jail time.[104] French privacy laws state that parents are responsible for protecting images of children. Under the law, grown-up children could potentially sue their parents for pictures posted when they were younger. French police warn parents about the danger of pedophiles targeting children online or criminals stealing pictures to use for identity theft.

Government officials in the UK are looking to propose Internet Rights, referred to as "Irights" for those under 18. Under the UK plan, young people will have the right to demand that any pictures or information about them online be deleted.[105] [106]

Websites will be encouraged to have a delete button to prevent embarrassing or compromising photos or information being stored online. The European Union is also proposing regulations referred to as "the right to erasure" allowing

104. Fox8WEBCENTRAL (2016, March 3) *Parents in France could face jail time, fines for posting photos of their kids on social media*. Retrieved from: http://fox8.com/2016/03/03/parents-in-france-could-face-jail-time-fines-for-posting-photos-of-their-kids-on-social-media/

105. Peev, G. (2015, July 28) *Let children delete embarrassing photos from web: Ministers back ex-Facebook boss's call for 'iRights'* Mail Online. Retrieved from: http://www.dailymail.co.uk/news/article-3176685/Ministers-ex-Facebook-boss-s-call-iRights-let-children-delete-embarrassing-photos-web.html

106. Ward, V. (2015, July 28) *Children should be able to delete photos from the web*. The Telegraph. Retrieved from: http://www.telegraph.co.uk/technology/11767182/Children-should-be-able-to-delete-photos-from-the-web.html

adults to demand any images posted by them when they
were under 18 be deleted.

"Digital Kidnapping"

There is a disturbing trend happening on social media
referred to as "Digital Kidnapping" where people steal
online photos of children and reshare the photos as if the
children were their own.[107] It's a type of online "baby role
play" in which people create new fictional lives and identities for the digital kidnapped child. There are even hash-
tags creating communities around online "baby roll play"
where users pretend to be the parent or the child and add
to the story line. Although the intentions are not always
malicious, some role players act out sexual fantasies with
the kidnapped photos adding to this disturbing trend.

The scary reality is that once you upload a photo you have
no control over where it could end up. So what can parents do? Experts say that before sharing a photo online
make sure that there are no details that could help a stran-
ger identify the location of your child. Gary Davis (Intel
Security's chief consumer safety evangelist) suggests parents download an app that watermarks personal photos so
no one else can claim them as their own. He also says never
add location tags to your photos. If there are other children
in the photo, ask permission from their parents before
posting. Try to avoid tagging friends and family in photos
because that only spreads the photos to more and more
people which means less control over them. And finally,

107. Friedman M. (2015, July 31) *"Digital Kidnapping" Is a Real (and Creepy) Threat When You Post Your Children's Photos Online.* Retrieved from Woman's Day website: http://www.womans-day.com/relationships/family-friends/news/a51374/digital-kidnapping/

make sure your privacy settings are on the strictest possible settings. If you are still concerned about digital kidnapping, you could always email or text photos to friends and family members.

CHAPTER ELEVEN

Real World or Virtual World; Where Do You Live?

konstantynov@123RF.com

S ocial media has blurred the line between the real world and virtual world. Nowadays it seems that many people enjoy living in the virtual world more than the real world. It's important to recognize the realities of the virtual world.

Virtual World Realities

Not Everything is Real or True

Ioulia Bolchakova@123RF.com

In the virtual world anyone can be whatever they want to be and convince others that they are that person. The virtual world can convince young people that they are chatting with someone their own age, when in fact it's a sexual predator, putting them in grave danger. The virtual world can convince a young person that their life is not worth living.

The virtual world can also convince an adult that they have found the love of their life. In an elaborate online trend called "Catfishing," scammers create false online identities to lure people into romantic relationships.[108]

The term was first introduced in the 2010 movie "Catfish," an American documentary about a young man who builds an online relationship with a "young woman" on Facebook.

108. Peterson, Hayley (Jan 17, 2013) *'Catfishing:' The phenomenon of Internet scammers who fabricate online identities and entire social circles to trick people into romantic relationships*. The Daily Mail Online. Retrieved from: http://www.dailymail.co.uk/news/article-2264053/Catfishing-The-phenomenon-Internet-scammers-fabricate-online-identities-entire-social-circles-trick-people-romantic-relationships.html

He soon discovers that she is a middle-aged wife and mother. The movie has since led to a popular reality TV series. Catfish scammers use someone else's pictures and create fake profiles to attract people who are looking for romance. They have no intention of cultivating a romance in the real world—many just enjoy the online role play and will always find excuses for why they can't meet in person or provide more specific information. In an even more disturbing trend, many lonely adults have been the target of a type of catfishing where their "online lover" convinces them to send money for a wide variety of false reasons. This can go on for years, and many victims have found themselves in financial ruins because of the catfishing scheme. Inevitably, this leads to heartbreak, stress and possible mental health issues. Vulnerability and social media is a bad combination. Vulnerability refers to a person's risk of being hurt. Talk to trusted friends and family in the real world for emotional support.

Virtual Becoming Reality

Jozef Polc@123RF.com

As virtual reality continues to rapidly develop (blurring the line between reality and fantasy), it will become more challenging to distinguish between the real world and virtual world, and fight the attraction to escape reality for a fantasy experience. All signs point towards a future with virtual reality. People may prefer to spend the majority of their time in the virtual world where they are able to immerse themselves in 3D lifelike experiences. Some fear that we may become a society of "virtual humans." According to Dr. Elias Aboujaoude, a Stanford psychiatrist and author of *Virtually You, The Dangerous Powers of the E-Personality*, virtual reality may drastically change a person's emotional and social needs over time. "We may stop needing or craving real social interactions because they may become foreign to us." She also notes that people who report a high level of fulfillment from virtual reality experiences often have underlying conditions such as untreated social anxiety. Even though not all people who enjoy virtual reality experiences have underlying mental health conditions, it is something to be aware of. Remember only the real world can meet your emotional and social needs. The virtual world is a nice place to visit, but you don't want to live there.

Cyberbullying

Lorelyn Medina@123RF.com

Cyberbullying is when a child or teen becomes a target of actions by others using computers, cellphones or other devices that are intended to embarrass, humiliate, torment, threaten or harass. It can start as early as age eight or nine, but the majority of cyberbullying takes place in the teenage years, up to age 17.[109] Cyberbullying can be emotionally damaging, causing serious mental health issues and could lead to tragic consequences. We are all aware of how cyberbullying has contributed to far too many youth suicides. It shows how power-

---

109. Government of Canada (2015, July, 7) *What is cyberbullying?* Retrieved from: http://www.getcybersafe.gc.ca/cnt/cbrbllng/prnts/cbrbllng-en.aspx

ful social media can be, to be able to convince a young person that their life is not worth living. Close to 10% of teens have been victims of online bullying on social networking sites (Ipsos 2013).[110] Unlike face to face bullying, cyberbullying is sustained and repeated over a period of time and can spread very quickly. It can reach a victim anywhere at any time.

In a 2012 Angus Reid public opinion poll, 65% of Canadians think bullying should be considered a crime even if no physical violence is involved, and 90% would make it illegal to use electronic means to "coerce, intimidate, harass or cause other substantial emotional distress." [111]

Even though there is an increasing number of "Stop Bullying" campaigns, it still continues to happen, which is why it's important for parents and youth to learn strategies on how to prevent cyberbullying.

Cyberbullying: Prevention Tips for Parents and Teens

Tips for Parents

Have a Discussion with Your Child About Cyberbullying

Reassure them you won't take away their social networking access or mobile device. Children and teens are often afraid to confide in their parents for fear their online access or devices will be taken away.

---

110. (2013) *Bullies Taking to Social Networking as Teens Become More Mobile.* Retrieved from http://www.ipsos-na.com/news-polls/pressrelease.aspx?id=6010

111. Angus Reid (2012, February 29). *Many Canadians Believe Bullying Should Be Considered a Crime.* Retrieved from Angus Reid Global website: http://angusreidglobal.com/wp-content/uploads/2012/02/2012.02.29_Bullying_CAN.pdf

Be Careful Not to Interrogate, Be a Good Listener

Ask open ended questions and take your lead from their answers.

Know what Sites Your Kids are On

It's important to learn what sites your kids are on and what they do online. Know the technology and keep up with it.

Refer to Recent Stories in the News

This will show that you are aware of the importance of the subject and will help open up the lines of communication.

Ask About Any Personal Experience

This will give them an opportunity to share about a friend's experience, or even open up about their own personal experience.

Tips for Teens

Do Not Retaliate or Respond to the Cyberbullying

Bullies crave attention, and replying to them gives them attention and more power and reinforces that cyberbullying is okay.

Report the Online Bullying to the Social Media Site it Happened On

Most social media sites have policies against abuse, and whoever violates those policies will likely get notified and prevented from using that site.

Keep a Record of the Cyberbullying

Save all messages, comments and posts as evidence.

Block the Person Doing the Bullying

This is one of the most effective ways to stop cyberbullying early.

Tell Someone; Remember You are Not Alone

Talk to a teacher or a parent immediately before it escalates. A parent can guide you and support you through the process of stopping the bullying.

If you are aware of someone who is being bullied online or in person and don't do anything about it, studies show that you could experience the "Bystander Effect," which is when individuals do not offer any help to a victim when other people are present. Social psychologists Bibb Latané and John Darley first identified the bystander effect after conducting experiments in 1968 on how people reacted in different situations. The study was a response to a murder of a woman in New York in 1964, where 38 people witnessed the crime from their apartment windows, but no one tried to help the victim or even call police.

The bystander effect could promote bullying.[112] Bullies like to have a passive audience, but will most likely stop if there is disapproval from the audience, but a person should only intervene if it is absolutely safe to do so. The bystander effect may also have physical and emotional ramifications. Researchers at Pennsylvania State University found that

---

112. NoBulling.com.(2014, June 12.) *How the Bystander Effect Could Promote Bullying.* Retrieved from: http://nobulling.com/how-the-bystander-effect-could-promote-bullying/

children who repeatedly witness bullying may suffer physical and emotional trauma and have difficulty acquiring a sense of safety and affiliation with others, which could last for years after bullying events.[113]

Some of the bystander fears include: afraid of becoming the next victim, not knowing what to do, or fear of being labelled a "snitch."

When it comes to bullying in the real world or the virtual world:

Record It — Report It — Don't Support It

For immediate support call the **Kids Help Phone**:
1 (800) 668-6868

For more information on how to be cyber safe visit
www.getcybersafe.gc.ca

Real World Benefits

Social media has created a virtual world that has become like a drug that some people are now addicted to. Like most drug addicts, you believe it will ease your pain and take you to a fantasy place where you can forget your troubles for awhile. You now believe you can be whoever you want. You can invite other addicts to be your "FRIEND," "LIKE" and "FOLLOW" you. You have escaped your real world problems. But remember, eventually you have to come back to your reality where your real world issues still exist.

The real world is where your true friends are, who like you for who you are and will truly be there when you need

---

113. Penn State News. (2011, Oct. 11) *Study shows bullying affects both bystanders and target.* Retrieved from: http://news.psu.edu/story/154651/2011/10/11/study-shows-bullying-affects-both-bystanders-and-target

them; friends who will laugh with you rather than just text LOL, friends who will notice your real sad face and provide comfort and support, friends who will give you real hugs instead of virtual ones.

CHAPTER TWELVE

Stop Capturing and Live in the Moment

Dmytro Panchenko@123RF.com   rdonar@123RF.com

Technology allows us to record our day-to-day experiences easier than ever before. Just look around and notice all the people viewing life through the screen of a smartphone camera. Before smartphones, film had to be developed at a cost, so you were careful about how many pictures you took. You would take your picture and move on. You would spend more time living the moments than capturing the moments. Nowadays it's the opposite. People are spending more time capturing the moments than living the moments. People will pay hundreds of dollars on a concert and then end up spending most of the time looking through the tiny screen on their phone to record it, totally missing out on the complete visual experience. And if not the tiny screen on a phone, the large screen at the concert. We are so attracted to technology that we are drawn to watching the large video screen at a concert rather than viewing the stage with our own eyes. Viewing the stage with our own eyes allows us to capture what we want to capture, rather than having someone dictate that for us.

How Smartphones Can Impair Memory

Taking a photo or a video is all about saving memories, but research has shown that smartphones could actually be impairing our memories of those special moments. Linda A. Henkel from the Department of Psychology at Fairfield University in Connecticut conducted a study on how taking photographs shapes our memories.[114] [115] The study included sending groups of students to the university's art museum. The students observed some objects and photographed others. The next day their memory was tested. They recalled more details about the objects they did not photograph and were worse at recognizing and recalling details of the objects they had photographed. Henkel describes it as "photo-taking impairment effect." She says her students' memories were impaired because the camera acts as an external memory aid that we count on to remember the details. "As soon as you hit 'click' on that camera, it's as if you've outsourced your memory," she says. "Any time we count on these external memory devices, we're taking away from the kind of mental cognitive processing that might help us actually remember that stuff on our own." So the more we record, the less we actually remember. She doesn't recommend that we stop taking photos, but what

114. Henkel, L.A. (2014, February 7) *Point-and-Shoot Memories: The Influence of Taking Photos on Memory for a Museum Tour.* Retrieved from Psychological science journal website: http://pss. sagepub.com/content/early/2013/12/04/0956797613504438.abstract

115. Meyer, A. (2014, March 3) Psychology Today. *Taking Pictures Might Impair Your Memory.* Retrieved from: https://www.psychologytoday.com/blog/c-is-cognition/201403/taking-pictures-might-impair-your-memory

she does recommend is to be more mindful when taking pictures and to realize that a picture is just a snapshot of a memory. She states that human memory is much more dynamic than photographs. Photos remain the same every time you look at them, but memories change over time.

Psychologist Dr. Rick Norris is convinced that obsessive documentation is detrimental to our experiences. He states vision is our dominant sense, but we also have four others, and living in the moment, rather than focusing on capturing it, utilizes all of our senses so the experience becomes much more memorable.[116] Recording a moment leaves us with something that will trigger a memory in the future, but if it was experienced through a screen in the first place, then it won't be as strong. Try not to focus so much on capturing the moment with your smartphone camera. A lot of time can be spent taking photos and videos that just end up in a virtual file that is hardly ever viewed. Live in the moment and capture it with your real world senses.

---

116. Halliwell, R. (2014, November 13). *Stop recording and start living in the moment*. Retrieved from *The Telegraph* website: http://www.telegraph.co.uk/sponsored/finance/personal-economy/11213193/start-living-in-the-moment.html

CHAPTER THIRTEEN

Be Aware and Always Read Your "Warning Label"

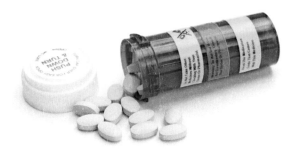

Sherry Yates Young@123RF.com

I believe everyone needs reminders from time to time about anything in life that has the potential to cause mental or physical harm. It's important to share your feelings and emotions rather than keeping them bottled up inside. Don't use emoticons or emojis as the only way to express your feelings and emotions. Be honest and open about feelings of anxiety and depression with trusted friends and family members, and seek help if you notice that symptoms are lingering. If you're in crisis, call 911 or head to the nearest hospital emergency room.

It's a miracle I am alive today. I could have easily become an alcoholic, drug addict or suicide statistic. I reached for help and so can you. There is no shame in asking for help.

It will be the best decision you will ever make for yourself and those close to you.

Social Media Positives

Not everything about social media is negative, it's important to recognize some of the positives.

- Connection to the world for locating people, jobs and news stories.

- Immediate information gathering, sharing and networking.

- Inexpensive way to market products and services to world-wide consumers.

- It's constantly evolving; you become more familiar with new and emerging technologies.

- Exposes you to many new viewpoints, ideas, and opinions that you may not be familiar with and allows you to share yours.

- Keeps you in touch with family members and friends that live far away.

- Create an immediate call to action for an event or cause.

Hitting the "Reality Button"

The reality is—the internet and all it has to offer will continue to evolve with new features to attract users. Trying to keep up with new technology can be very time consuming and expensive (which could cause family issues and anxiety). When a new product comes out there is plenty of hype that many people get caught up in, causing them to get up early in the morning and stand in line for hours to try to get the latest technological advancement, but it doesn't take very long for that product to become "old" technology. In most cases the manufacturer already has the next device ready to go when the current model is released. So it can become an anxiety induced fixation for having the "latest" technology.

You should ask yourself—what is motivating me to want the latest? Is because of the hype created and the feeling of FOMO (fear of missing out) and keeping up with your friends and family? It seems the message consumers are getting from manufacturers is—don't settle for what you have, get the latest and greatest now!

We can't turn back the clock to a time when technology was simpler with no internet, social media or smart phones trying to grab our attention 24/7. The world is always changing, and for the most part that's a good thing. Technology and specifically the internet have changed our world. It's made the world more accessible for reaching out, gathering and sharing information, expressing opinions and more. If controlled and used effectively, it can enhance our lives. Evolving technology can be exciting and very useful. Try to control your desire to keep up and recognize what is motivating you, which should be based on *your* individual needs rather than what *other* people say you need.

Be conscious of the things in life that could affect your mental health, and if issues arise seek support in the real world. Be aware of the social media drug; it can be very addictive and comes with an unlimited amount of refills. But unfortunately it doesn't come with a warning label. You need to create your own warning label based on *your* feelings and emotions. Use social media wisely and hit the reality button from time to time.

Alphabetical Index of Topics

To order more copies of this book visit **www.wadesorochan.com**

To find books by other Canadian authors, or make inquiries about publishing your own book, contact PageMaster at:

PageMaster Publication Services Inc.
11340-120 Street, Edmonton, AB T5G 0W5
books@pagemaster.ca
780-425-9303
catalogue and e-commerce store www.PageMasterPublishing.ca/Shop

About the Author

Wade Sorochan is a well-known radio personality in Edmonton, Alberta, Canada. Wade first gained recognition for his pioneering impact on the number one rated and "Canada's most unique" radio talk show *The Bill & Bill Show*. Nicknamed "The Tone Arm," Wade became the first broadcaster in history to use music to enhance a radio talk show. Wade went on to produce and host his own popular radio talk shows *Life Talk with Wade Sorochan* and *Edmonton This Week*. Wade Sorochan has interviewed numerous celebrities, politicians and everyday people for over 35 years and is recognized as one of the best interviewers in the business and a talk show pioneer.

Wade Sorochan is the owner of his own communications company providing freelance broadcasting, event hosting, and motivational speaking. As a mental illness survivor, Wade is a sought after motivational speaker sharing his inspiring personal story of living with mental illness at numerous events, including the 2011 International Symposium on Wellness. Wade has been recognized as a nominee for the Alberta Lieutenant Governor's True Grit Award for *"Excellent Work to Strengthen Outcomes and Quality of Life for People Living with Mental Illness and Addiction."*

Contact and booking information available at:

www.wadesorochan.com